Gunpowder Valentine

First published in 2014 by
The Dedalus Press
13 Moyclare Road
Baldoyle
Dublin 13
Ireland

www.dedaluspress.com

ISBN 978 1 906614 94 2

Dedalus Press titles are represented in the UK by
Central Books, 99 Wallis Road, London E9 5LN
and in North America by Syracuse University Press, Inc.,
621 Skytop Road, Suite 110, Syracuse, New York 13244.

Cover image by Eric Roux-Fontaine
www.rouxfontaine.com

The Dedalus Press receives financial assistance from
The Arts Council / An Chomhairle Ealaíon

Gunpowder Valentine

New and Selected Poems

Paul Perry

DEDALUS PRESS
DUBLIN, IRELAND

ACKNOWLEDGEMENTS

Grateful Acknowledgment is made to The Arts Council of Ireland for a Literature Bursary, 2011 and to Salmon Poetry who first published *The Drowning of the Saints*, and to Dún Laoghaire-Rathdown County Council and Dún Laoghaire-Rathown Library Services who made the publication of *108* Moons possible. Original versions of poems from *108* Moons were translated from the Lithuanian with Ruta Suchodolskyte. Thanks to the editors of the following publications where some of the poems from Gunpowder Valentine an first appeared: *The Irish Times, Poetry Ireland Review*, the Upstart Campaign, a non-profit arts collective aimed at putting creativity at the centre of public consciousness during the Irish General Election Campaign of *February, 2011, Upstart Blog, EYEWEAR, The Burning Bush 2 & 3, Airborne: Poetry from Ireland*, edited by Pat Boran (iBooks platform, Dedalus Press, 2011) and If Ever You Go: A Map of Dublin in Poetry and Song, edited by Pat Boran and Gerard Smyth (Dedalus Press, 2014).

Contents

*

'How is it possible to want so many things
and still want nothing.'
— Stephen Dobyns, *How to Like it*

for Aoife, Bláithín, Fionn and Leonora

Introduction

*

A PAUL PERRY POEM extends an invitation to the reader – we are not left out in the cold, but are invited in to see what he sees, whether that's the 'elegant shabbery' of a five-bar gate, later bought by a woman 'with a wallet', or the vagaries of love, loss and argument. We become implicated readily, and this honesty of feeling, unusual in the contemporary poem, is what marks this volume of new and selected work.

There's an expansiveness of scope here, allowing for poems that emerge from the long view of history and others which re-work folk legend into parables for our times. Darker moments show a restless spirit that speaks to the variance of form and of poetics, now observable in selections from the earlier books presented alongside the new work of *Gunpowder Valentine*. Perry's world is the compromised, chastened, technology-loving world we live in but he manages to convey that it is not reduced, flattened or less than it was. There's no nostalgia here, instead a sometimes headlong sense of passionate engagement.

The breadth of horizon, reminiscent of Whitman and the forensic wit, worthy of a Stevens, indicates a lyric ability that has been honed by interaction with the expressive poetic traditions of the United States. The result is an all-encompassing sense of the world as not too big, too multiple, too nefarious to be confronted by art, but rather that the poem is capacious enough, various enough and important enough to do that work.

Many poems assert themselves as meditations, ruminative yet peppered with striking images. The testing of received ideas leads to a playfulness with language and sometimes to a celebratory note which feels all the more earned because of what has gone before.

In *The Drowning of the Saints* (2003), we are introduced to memory as a method of 'telling' the layered histories of those who strive, a mode noted as not necessarily reliable but certainly able to provide psychological truth. There's a sense of the loss of the ceremonial blessing of organised religion:

> Standing over the fox's body
> with no benediction other than the thought
>
> that things are passing from our lives.'
> 'Red dogs of Wicklow'

Poems like 'Of the gas stove and the glimmerman' take account of the human cost of historic positioning on the island of Ireland while a grander gesture is invoked in pieces which take their cue from nature, 'the owl calls out like a gaping heart'. Here is a poet who risks the romantic, who makes readers understand that the poem itself can hold a multitude, that even in dark times we might feel the 'small heartbeat of forgiving'. 'The Walk' might be a coda to the development of a poet, a portrait of the artist as a younger man:

> we took a walk
> and grew too big for the town

or, as he has it in 'The Gate to Mulcahy's Farm', 'Perhaps this is another version of heaven' and we see the poet as a construer of those other versions, with a healthy respect for the transformative power of imagination.

In *The Orchid Keeper* (2006), we meet a writer who in the act of 'getting ready for the cold, its indiscretion, its disregard', suggests with quiet insistence that we 'be nothing less than amazed'. We meet the poet on the cusp of the modernist project, both wistful and aware, both romantic and constructivist, and with a sense of how the stuff of the poem will operate on the reader. This is one of Perry's gifts. As Fred D'Aguiar has remarked, 'Like W.S. Merwin, Mr. Perry seems to have a unique talent for closing lines that open numerous possibilities of meaning while suggesting something absolute.'

We are asked to 'imagine the driver concussed' in a striking fable, 'Ode to a Car Crash' where the reader may be aligned with the 'shadow driver', the one who effectively drives the poem in a flipped-eye view. Reality encountered through this artistic prism is where we see 'a negative / all light' and learn that we may be 'a caretaker ... of sorts' minding the 'car's altar' where the whole scope of a life is adumbrated. In the end, 'the engine is removed / transplanted' and we are asked to rise to the challenge of this work as such or be left 'pointing all the way to eternity'.

Elsewhere in this section, poems with tightly wound couplets culminate in 'Towing an Iceberg to Belfast' where we are reminded that 'All poetry is performance / All poetry is L=A=N=G=U=A=G=E' in a piece that presents the writing of poetry as a small stay against the recent history of the island, 'It is agreed / All poems are to be decommissioned', while at the same time the image of the iceberg and its unlikely arrival in Belfast, become the lasting imaginative gifts of the piece, proving the point the poet is making.

The selection from this book ends with a poem 'Variation on the word love' which has the making of art as its subject as well as love and loss-making. Here is the presence of the author, disarmingly honest or so it appears: 'I'm scared sometimes / of the unexplored caverns of the mind' leaving the poem itself as the image in which we see ourselves, 'lying in a field and someone/is calling out your name / and it's snowing'.

The work in *108 Moons* (2009) is rendered with a shorter, sometimes staccato line with striking pictorial moments and a sense of allegorical import driven by an almost magical realism. The poems in this section may be singing initially from the atmosphere of their gestation in creative translation from the Lithuanian and they move outward from there to the Tibetan 'Glass Mountain' where fittingly, 'All boundaries overflow'.

Throwing other work into relief, we see now that a project which did not seem 'Irish' as such has nonetheless been necessarily driven by a set of obsessions emanating from, but not confined to, the contested state. The poems in *108 Moons* act like an interlude where 'Nowhere is not a place, / but a gap between two words' while a piece like 'Blue Sparks' develops an oracular and haiku-like imagistic approach where the 'I' of the speaker becomes in effect, the readers' 'eye'.

A sense both of the fragility of love and of the wilful innocence that the poem itself must wield drives both the personal and political work in *The Last Falcon and Small Ordinance* (2010). Children have a presence in the aesthetic, welcomed as part of a knowing wish for fulfilment that unabashedly seeks both the beautiful and the true in lyrics like 'First Night': 'how frightened I was / before you were delivered / tugged-tired from your mother'. There is a sense, building on earlier work, of love as a stay against human conflict, where it may make a place to say 'wars are not your concern'. Perry displays a technical mastery of the dismantled love poem, warning us via linguistic riffs and surprising shifts of focus that the contemporary poem must deal with the modernist legacy, must operate with a sense of its own artifice. He draws attention to the texture of the words and to how they operate beyond meaning as well as deftly using the idea of multiple 'tellings' as a counterpoint to the closed tradition of the 'told'.

This most recent book joins the new work of *Gunpowder Valentine* in a particular aesthetic moment. With an understanding that 'everything is present', Perry takes on the modern project, at times proffering work akin to process-poetry (the poetry of the poem revealing its own becoming) while managing to draw the reader into that process. Here is a poet who uses many poetic modes as if to posit that a writer should not just support the associative, the linguistically playful or the elliptical but choose a form for each discrete act of making. The humility in the face of the art that is necessary to do this is palpable throughout and particularly so in the poems of social commitment. The advantage of a selected volume is that we can observe from a privileged position. In this recent work, much has occurred outside the 'happening' of the poem but as we encounter work that begins in medias res, we've been trained as readers to keep up with this restless intelligence, the engine of the ethical engagement with the pressing questions of our time.

In *Gunpowder Valentine,* from the title poem which exerts a mesmeric force, this is work that speaks to times of societal pressure, to present-day fear of violence and to the historical legacy of political violence. Even 'the rivers are our enemies' where 'picking strawberries is not allowed'. Here the poem is used for exploring the machinations of political control, but it still retains the lyric form and posits musical power as an antidote. In re-worked folk tale and legend, what happens 'in the forest in the forest in the forest' implies a sense of shared humanity and shared quest, the humanist ideal which operates to fuel this poetry. Children, young people, the loneliness of soldiering — all come within the gambit of the Perry gaze. In 'To the Republic', Perry gives us a hint that the idea of a true republic, not just Plato's but Kant's, provides a backdrop to this meditative sequence of poems. Even here however, a serious playfulness is in order as in the sequence using the persona of Lugh where we wonder which façade to encounter first — sun god or trickster, lightning flash or strong-arm?

Perry forces us to think about our place in the world, to take a stance, to engage with the poem which will not provide closure but an opening, a chink through which to observe the lived life. In this sense he is a moralist, but in the subtlest form, demanding that we join in his powerful statement of what poetry can do and why this art is essential.

— Siobhán Campbell
2013

Gunpowder Valentine

Gunpowder Valentine

I.

I went there too
I did not have to go
I saw the best of men

clearing the villages was awful
we hated ourselves for that
in the streets we found

maddened cows dripping
with milk
bellowing in pain

it was something terrible
I saw a cat in a window
I thought it was an ornament

then I saw that it was alive
I killed the cat
I got used to killing

forgive us
we found notes nailed
to the doors of houses

be careful we'll be back
don't kill our cat
our house we are sorry

for leaving you
cold and alone
I came home

my wife was frightened
she insisted I throw my clothes away
I did that

all except for my hat
it had a badge on the front
and my son I knew would like it

he was proud of me
he went around wearing this hat
some nights he wore it in bed

one year after that time
he fell ill
it was a brain tumour

that was it
I can say
no more

II.

I dream about it every night
we arrived at 6 a.m.
we told them to leave everything

they cried
as if they knew
they would never return

they offered us moonshine
everything was negotiable
we bartered cattle

they were sold cheap
Nature was dying
the houses were like works of art

empty now
the shadow of madness
was on us all

III.

we lifted the topsoil

the burial grounds were open pits

we stripped the earth and orchard

do not have children they told us

at night we drank

we drank hard

we slept in beds of straw

IV.

we gathered at the train station
it was May
we had been chosen

our work was secret
the mood was fun
we were conscripts

and were called tourists
from the trains we saw the fields
change from green

to something more lunar
white dolomite sand covered
miles of field where the green

earth had once been
we knew then something
was very wrong

the roofs had the names of women
Katya Natasha Anna
Marsha was the mad one

she was cut open like a wound
we stopped laughing
after we arrived in hell

V.

they bent to the water
but did not drink

VI.

the garden all dressed
in wedding white
my hives over there

under the apple trees
I said to Nina my wife
what's wrong

I put on my mask
and checked
they were there

sitting in the hives
not making a sound
there was no buzzing

so strange was their silence

VII.

the rain was black
and one by one the children fell
I will never forget the mornings

the girls had ribbons in their hair
the boys wore shorts
inside I am empty

I have seen and heard too much
I was happy once
the children came from love

our lives are a long winter
without spring
we bury our children's clothes in the dirt

VIII.

we came carrying birch and rowan
a storm broke
dust entered our mouths and eyes
like a black wing
we went on singing
the rivers are our enemies
picking strawberries is not allowed
or bluebells or daisies or mushrooms
the village is buried
in a bitter dream

For two NATO soldiers who drowned in an attempt to recover supplies from a river in the province of Badghis, Western Afghanistan, November 2009

two boys lie
head down
in water

turning
like the hands
of a dial

they make up
the body
of a cold clock

their winter numbers
frozen
no alarm-bell

rings out
no shock is captured
in the atmosphere

nor is it known
how suddenly
they fell

into the water's gasp
or how quickly
they succumbed

to the icy
verisimilitude
their pale still

faces drawn
towards the bottom
their eyes starless

and threadbare
emerging
from the corner

of one mouth
a delicate bead of air
from the other

nothing —

at dawn
I fill
their pockets

then rinse
their hands
with light

A Presidential Epigram

after Mandelstam

we live without feeling
the border between us

and our feet do not touch the ground

listen —
our voices are accent-less
and the echo of money
is like the sound of rigging in the wind

the talk of any small-town is the Áras
and the one who chuckles

shall he ascend —
his bloodied hands unseen
boots put away
worms rising

his words are like anchors

circled by snivelling and mewling henchmen
he flings decrees like horseshoes —
you get it in the balls
the temple
between eyes

like poisoned berries
he spits each execution from his mouth

The River Merchant: A Reply

Five months have passed my love and more and still I have not made it to Cho-fu-Sao. Chokan is a dream to me now though I can see you as something real, hear your voice, taste its small insistence. Sometimes I think these words will not be read. It makes me want to say the saddest things. It makes me want to say: hold fast my love, show thyself simple, preserve thee pure. Live in the fruit, not the flower.

I am returning. I have always been returning. You know that now as once you knew me by my bamboo stilts, but the days are not long enough or too long and ... where am I now? Have you climbed the look out? And when? And how many times before our dust is mingled? Before ... but wait, let me tell you this, let me tell you what I have seen: sun, the wind, the gentle wind and a flight of dragons without heads. I climbed the nine hills and saw the strange fish in the well.

The town may be changed, but the well cannot be changed. Five months have passed my love and more and still I have not made it to Cho-fu-Sao. I am returning. I have always been returning. Sometimes I think these words will not be read. Sun, the wind, the gentle wind and a flight of dragons without heads. This is what I have learned: even a lean pig has it in him to rage around.

There is no skin on my thighs and walking comes hard. I shot fish at the well-hole, my love. Live in the fruit, not the flower. You know that now as once you knew me by my bamboo stilts. The jug is broken and leaks. No animals come to an old well. I did not drink the mud of the well. This is my heart's sorrow, for I might have drawn from it. If the king were clear-minded, if the king ... Five months have passed my love and more. I am mindful of the danger, and no great mistake is made. One day I found a melon covered with willow leaves. Live in the fruit ... have you climbed the look out? And when? It makes me want to say the saddest things. The jug is broken and leaks. And still I have not made it to Cho-fu-Sao. Even a lean pig has it in him to rage around. Chokan is a dream to me now.

I climbed the nine hills am mindful of the danger. So take this brooch then as a symbol of my love. You know that now as once you knew me. Five months have passed my love and more. If the king were clear-minded, if the king ... hold fast my love and but wait, and let me tell you this: if I come with horns or you do not know me, I am returning, I have always been, this is my heart's sorrow — think of the sun, the wind, the gentle wind and place the brooch within the yellow chrysanthemums and hold them to the flame.

Mr. Hansel, Mr. Gretel

in the forest in the forest in the forest in the forest in the forest
where you were sent to eat to drink to sit and wait to perish
farther darker deeper into time my time no time your mother's
womb expelled and where I she anyway no one seems to know
but I do might have once before the other came from the forest

with rain with rain with rain with rain with rain amen
soil beneath her fingernails ice in her hair her eyes
made from November and when she touched me I
came to life and swore I had never known or begat what not
or they that cried and huddled and famished sent to

the centre the centre the centre the centre the centre
where the river ends and the voices stop and the moon
the moon it does nothing but announces night and winter
and lights no one's way because she will have her say and
you your body grows too fast and needs too much

of home of home of home of home of home
where I waited for you only to send you back
only to wait for you only to love you more than I could
only to hold you to save you by speaking your names
buried beneath with with with who who her yes

in the forest the forest the forest the forest the forest

Jesus as a young Hungarian deaf woman circa. 1940

The windows were tiny and the train started.
At night the train stopped.
We got off.

We lay down in a huge yard.
We received this uniform, put a kerchief on our heads;
everybody retained their shoes.

It was odd to be bald.
Everybody was very cold.
I got scared because I found some lice.

It was strange.
The other women's legs were swollen.
We were working in the mud,

Sweeping the area in January.
There were officers sitting at a table —
My sister warned me.

Somebody said, "Don't you like the deaf?"
I said, "I listen to my sister."
I was sent out to dig the graves.

I was the 'crier'.
My hands were hurting ...
It was cold.

I wasn't strong.
My sister was much stronger than me.
I was digging the graves.

We were fighting.
We stole from each other.
The last grave I dug was my own.

To the Republic

after Frank Bidart

imagine they picked themselves up
from the ground
from where they had fallen
dipped their hands into their wounds
and pulled out the fire-wear
which had entered them by decree
imagine they un-strapped the other
from the chair he had rested in
righted him and put their shoulders
beneath his arms and carried him
imagine they walked through our city again
what a parade it would be
we might stand about in disbelief
take pictures or lower our eyes in shame —
poets come back to life
give us our daily bread

I Am Lugh

I am Lugh. I sleep like the dead
My bed is a rolling wave
I roll. I sink. I rise again
I was a warrior, worrier,
Wannamaker —
I was one of them too to think on it
With rice in my mouth
Or my thumb stretched out
I'm still getting used to my second life
Refining the shit-eating grin on my avatar
When xmas comes and it does — I plan
To reincarnate: I may come in disguise
But I am always in disguise
And do not know anyway
What form my incarnation will take
Even my children do not recognise me
Especially when I wake and tell them
How much I have missed them
How much I love them still

Lugh as the Wolf

I also had a mother
she suckled me
before I left

I did not know the way
I hid in culverts and thickets
friendless but for an owl

I am a wolf waiting
the shadows know my tread
that is me gliding over the forest-floor

the house knows me too
the door is always open
the bed is made

and the girl who walks in
with her basket
she knows me by my name

L-aiku

Even in Dublin
hearing the trams
I long for Dublin

*

Dusk —
the foghorn quiet
forever now

fragrance sounds
night-struck
from chrysanthemums

*

The path to the park
is covered with leaves

when I left it was Spring

This December

my bed
a magic carpet
and
the curtains left
a little askew
onto Three Rock
and
as darkness
opened
I lay down
into the weave
and
exhaled
and watched
my breath
draw colour
from the hills
and watched
my father
and mother
grow small
from the toil
it had taken
to build
such a carpet
as this

few and far between

my father sat
across from me

at the table
he drank his tea

he ate his toast
I ran my spoon

about my bowl
our words were few

and far between
as they have always been

we had somewhere to go
or he had

at that age
it's all the same

but before we went
or got up to go

a crumb of bread
caught in his throat

and the drop of tea
he had supped

came unstuck
he coughed

he spluttered
a train of tea

came at me
my face was washed

with milky tea
and like all his kind

there was a sweetness to it
I wiped my face

with my hand
the back of

you understand
and looked to him

who I looked up to
always

once
smiling

saying
nothing

of much
consequence

August 30, 2012

desire's cost is soil soil soil
the house mirrored by a house house
buddleia cut down   bees fizz fizz
a robin red breast flits and flies
where is my nest was that my nest
a cat rakes through the new soil
mine is this mine territory mine
this is your life fleeting who needs money
or a father who stays on the island
who needs what no more kids so
a radio plays or is it the jingle of the TV news
TV
familiar childhood darkness
your mother is cleaning and cleaning and
cleaning and cleaning
international disappeared day
clean
what — everywhere in Ireland it's no seasons
seven remain the technology is there
a little bit of courage is all that's
have to keep on hoping
breath in my body keep asking
disappeared people people who know
who know where he is
nine of the disappeared won't give up
and so my mother is weeping and
and my brother wants a lift
lift lift home
he talks talks talks talks to himself
and says says says Ireland is an everywhere and
the heart heart heart is a rotten fruit and
we played at sticks as kids

and
we played at sticks as kids
and we moved moved moved moved moved
remember that house where we were happy
happy happy then ran away yes yes yes remember it well
the pain has grown like an unwatered plant
changing growing into and out of the soil
where desire's cost is a farewell where one man
is talking talking talking talking talking
to the wind wind wind wind wind
to the water water water water water
to the hah hah hah
hah hah hah
to the hah hah
hah hah

Lugh and Fionn

Two peas in a pod
And on their way to where
There's something of the son
In the father something
Which wants to sing
Five nine five nine
Did ever such a time
Ring true — he
A warrior whose stories
Preceded him — bed time
Tales to help us sleep
Together cheek to cheek
Or wrapped around each other
Like the lovers in some mythical romance

Variation on a Theme by Henry Buckle

in a given state of society
a certain number of persons
must
put an end
to their own irresistible fear
of another world
which is subordinate
to the special question:
who shall commit love

Lugh

after Brecht

I never thought
the simplest words
would be enough
when you say
what things are like
my heart is torn to shreds
when I don't
stand up for myself
I go down
I see that now

Gauguin on Three Rock

If I am the fox you will know

I am not after the bird between her fingers

my daughter would call it a spideog

the woman with the dark hair holds me

her feet are cold, her toes upcurled

cold blue eyes, her pain subsided

and I am transformed into the fox

this rusty paw on her breast says mine

this paw says and with whoever

you find you love you will not lie

or before the sun becomes your mourning

this paw says sorry and wish

this paw says if

but you must be cold

the sun is hidden

the field we lie on is brown

in the distance you can see the blue sea

green hills turn to red fields

you may not know but this is my first time too

what worries me

and I can see them out of the corner of my eye

are the people

who are they

townspeople, a mob, the woman's,

let's call her Rachel,

though she can never be Rachel again

her sister, family, people,

they come for me

because I have taken what cannot be given back

they are joined by children and vagabonds

the have blood in mind

I lick my paws

the bird in Rachel's fingers stirs

it's time we left

the soft wet earth

it's time we harried, hurried, fled

come now

the chaste sea beckons

our maiden descent

it's time we dressed

in whatever colours

the forest will lend us

Ticknock

From here the view of the city is a right
An undulating wasping chimera
Man on a hilltop
Or woman or child
As once I was bedded
In the mountain furze
Yielding
The city then is the grave
And the contours and slopes of the hills are its opposite
Magic and hidden and mythological
I am not the only one to say so
But I will be from now on
Let it be a protest and the rising hawk a sign
A flag of some kind of return
The cars career careen and un-sow
The seams of the hills
The city's spell broken
Rapacious — swarming with death
If after all the city is a grave
The wind moves through the forest
Smell of pine — up up up
Into the air into the past and future
Be here the stones cry
The mountains moving farther inland
The sea all roiling
Filial embrace like the noise
Of a blue light as if it were
A ship set sail lost unanchored
Making its way up to the foot of the hills
To the spine of whatever god has summoned us here

Lugh Considers Ireland — Ireland

1.

the sleep of an old oak tree the deftness of the graveyard the
sleep of a bird on a rolling wave shy eyes down your mouth
keeps coming blowing the moon the moon the moon if I slept
and talked and wept you would know I was not dead if the
dawn touches you like you want me to I will wake to the
sacrament of the flesh — did I sleep after all — and walk the
streets where fountains fall and oak trees lean where shy eyes
look to the bottom of a cold pool where we meet again for the
first time

2.

lost inside you my eyes full of emergency lost inside my hands
everywhere like the hooves of horses my eyes galloping towards
children we have loved

this sunflower is dying hold it for a moment ring its neck
because I am

3.

with all the water of the deepest lake you were a reed a swan a
bottle cap with all the sun and sky and clouds you were you
were you were the tree tops bed sheets hands tied you were lake
water a swan a reed

you were the sky the sky the sky

4.

who said what about you I I I between your lips a
hummingbird in your eyes something my memories don't
belong in your mouth but leave them there for the winter until
the punishment ends and if we dream let us dream and as for
your sorrow digress digress — give it a shape because a tongue
hunts it out like a dog a boy a boy an innocent the wind wants
us to give up if we are dead why do we love each other your
body yields it grows around me like a memory shifting wanting
speaking

Lugh Considers a Defence of Realism

involuntary   pine trees

yes   bulldozed and buried

yes   and twisted branches that do not reach for the sky

yes   o   and storks and wolves

yes   but not the dusky seaside sparrow

Harry Perry's Boxing Gloves

lie like two singing larks gone quiet:
Unlaced, bereft.

Sing again old friends,
Bloom; pucker for us one last time, won't you?

Lugh Considers the Paradox of the Raven

nothing can be a raven and not a raven
phenomenon is hostage
a raven is hostage
a raven is not hostage
hostage to nothing
a raven is nothing
a raven is not nothing
nothing can be a raven
nothing and not

Lugh Remembers the Whistle

stole it
buried it
not much to remember
I was a child
blew that whistle once
buried it in soil

told no one
nobody knew

it was summer-time

Lugh on the Wrack Line

I found your soul on the wrack line
        What was it doing there
I found your letters
        like tinder
        The words walking off the pages like tiny
ants
        your cowboy boots
        I found them too
                There was a big old radio
And in a haze of noise   were voices
        Our voices
        Reproachful tones
            Or loving notes
I can't be sure
                I found your shirt on the wrack line
        And the moon in a bucket
        And the blue dragonflies
        And wine stains
        And your smell was on the wrack line too
And the double rainbow
        You must have been there
                Because you are an animal
And like a fox you could tear the flesh of the face of a small child
        I found your memories there
                They shimmered in my hands
        On the wrack line
        In its sand and kelp
            Are we drowning
        Did we drown
            One of us
        Or are we

It is the only place we can
The only place
Its twilight here or dark
                I can see your shadow waning
Your tongue pulling me apart
                Undressing my soul
Your voice saturating the night
                You've built a small fire
I am the flint I am the ember I am the ash
        And I burn for you   Whisperings I hear whisperings
and   there have been murmurings too
We know it   of deaths   of murders of all manner of ...
        If like the rest of the debris
                If like the
        If
But you are quiet
                You wait   and the water you are scared of
Is that what is going on
        It was I
I wanted to swim in
                the heat of your body
What ship or boat or raft
                Did we fall from
        There was some kind of feast
If the light ever comes
                        Do you want it to
It must
                If the light
                What will you
Will you take my hand again
                                Because
        There is a storm
                It is coming but softly now
Rising and look at the water

Rising slowly but surely
And you know what that means
the wrack line
                        where I found you
Where you found me
                        broken
        But shining
The wrack line
        will be wrecked again and we
                we will be thrown against each other
                                        once more

Lugh Decides to Clone Himself

in case the world is too much
        or not enough
               in case I am childless
                  but I am not
in case I need to know
        where my doppelganger is
                  but I do
in case I want to interrogate myself
        and in the bright light of my double's moon
I shall suggest he leave
        go quickly without delay
               make what he can of this life
                  so spare and fleeting is it
        that if he stays he will perish surely

Lugh-a-law

Name: Lugh
    internet-savvy
transhuman leanings
      mac-inclined but without the means —
acorns fall into my hands when I say so —
       all the same I have been struck by lightning twice —
that's not the loving kind, by the way —
    slight twitch
          and a discernible limp
if you're looking for it
    I like waltzes by the river
       full moon charades
    comely maidenhood
and bi-location
    if it should come to it —
       at a crossroads
in short
    I know when to roll over
    but play dead?
not in this life time — not by your...

Lugh at Béal na Bláth

the clouds are full
      heavy bulging bloated

they receive this lord's head
             like a probe

the sound of electricity
      fizzes
             when stuck out
                   my tongue burns
         fingertips raw
             instead of speaking
        put this flower
             in your mouth

it will serve as our betrothal
                           it must

December 8th

wind —
the sound
of children's
voices —
a rumour
of poetry

from **The Drowning of the Saints**

Blessed is the fruit

Desolate apples, hold
tight in your bowl of water,
red, blushing, and blossoming light;

too big for the fruit bowl,
bitter pie stuff,
clean and eager

like some dowdy buoys
in a storm,
on say a Sunday,

and we wearing
our costumes,
not for mass,

but Halloween,
my brother remember is
something Frankensteinian

and I'm a ghost
dunking my head
into the cold

frivolous water
mouth open
like a dumb fish

in the depths —
childhood game;
apples, storm lights,

biblical beacons
of a lost faith,
first fruits, unforbidden,

but lost
like round unanchored
islands where we

returned after walking
from house to house
and trundling to and from the bonfire

to where the bowl,
like two clasped
plastic pale green hands,

a memory turned over,
lay with its bitten and chewed,
that is the yellowing skin of apple flesh

swelling sadly into the soft
unforgiven pulp
of all consumed

and discarded
temptations, though this
was the first, the first I remember.

The Red Dogs of Wicklow

We walked the long road to Templeogue.
Trees lined the street,

their rheumatic joints aching dampness and cold.
We found the fox with its dank head

in a puddle, the dark rusty bristles of its fur
hardening into the wind like old nails.

I wanted to lift it over the wall
into a field where the grass and leaves

would discolour into its skin as it fell asleep
into the soil, remembering the red dogs of Wicklow

and their snow felt steps into the dark, outside our door.
But we were hesitant, unsure, afraid of disease

and cold with rain. Standing over the fox's body
with no benediction other than the thought

that things are passing from our lives. And so,
we walked on, with our own small hurts

to contend with, until we turned from Terenure
to Templeogue and by some magic I looked

behind to see the fox alive and skulking by a tree,
darting off, it seemed, in every direction possible.

Of the gas stove and the glimmerman

I'll have to ask some questions in the kitchen
of the picture hanging in the hall, of the thin pointing nose
and gentle eyes. I'll have to ask some questions

of the civil servant, of the stranger
with nine children. You must have left suddenly
without warning even to yourself.

You must have gotten up early for work
and forgotten stupidly to come home.
Silly man. Your presence is a gasp.

She, on the other hand, never forgets
a birthday. Christmas presents for everyone.
She tours her children's houses

like a ring leader or a small storm,
nodding her head and spreading gossip,
singing a song or two and dancing once in a while.

She's gas; her eyes hold the best
part of a century. She'll tell you about the Black and Tans,
Dev, the gas stove and the glimmerman.

She watches out for us all,
but as for you old man,
people don't talk about the dead.

You have long fingers,
did you play the piano?
The picture, of course, is in black and white

so that is how I imagine you
a character in a black and white movie,
dumb, except for your twirling umbrella,

and the words you might have uttered,
caught in her memory, escaping only occasionally
like the startled bass from a torn fishing net.

I'll have to invite a slip of the tongue,
a nostalgic wink, or a hushed splutter.
Rathfarnham has changed.

You must not have known Stillorgan, the 46A,
the bus she takes or the bombs that still
wake us, the debris of our independence.

Your presence is a gasp.
I ask you if I should even bother
scribbling these questions.

'Write about the silence,' she says.
Old man,
you must not have known

she would have taken care of you,
or that when her mother died
my parents were away,

that she walked to our house
to take care of us, her grandchildren,
until my parents returned

and said to them simply and sternly,
'We buried my mother today.'
I think about my parents fighting

about which of their parents
was more patriotic,
the guns under the shopping trolley.

I think of the car crash
when my mother lost a child
and the galaxy of questions we live under,

the sheds with private conversations,
and I think of you, looking at her
ironing your daughter's skirts

and their long hair too
before they ran out the door
to school and her, again, pressing a wet cloth down

onto the hot stove and steam rising,
in black and white, whenever she heard the step
of the glimmerman come softly.

Rhapsody with Owl

the owl calls out like a gaping heart
and I am running plotting a getaway
through the wicklow fields
the building sites and lost wandering horses

maybe we knew they'd find us or maybe I did
or maybe my brother thought something different
maybe he really did think he'd get away
plotter and schemer that he was

with a black plastic bag
stuffed with jumpers and socks and jam sambos
my ankles were scabby and sore
from riding a new red bicycle I was sorry

to leave lying small and unconvinced
and shivering behind a bush
with no flames or sacrifice though the blackberries
were dripping with rain and that made them clean

and good to eat so that by the time
they found us our tongues were red like devils
my mother's car smelled of stale cigarette smoke
outside I smelled the freshly cut grass of summer

and heard the owl the dark glass sky
the fever the salt the thirst and colour
because the owl god of godless things
because the owl grass riddle glendalough

kilquade eight shadows from his mouth
because the owl feathered kafka glenmalure
airplanes and beetles candle flames
christ church no one is safe turned

around twice make any home your tree
any wind echo distance lack of water
or the sound thereof because the owl
black buddha of regret laughter in a well

small heart beat of forgiving wind thirst
salt the dark glass eye stars explode at your feet
the rain a dark web you are caught in
remember the sea is all around you

here is your past in a bowl take it
there is your future in the rain the sea
your face changed a thousand times into fire the soil
was red who are you petals of anger

in your palms lines paths I walked down
never turned left saw the rain and stars
death was on your lips on your tongue
in the air under rocks in the water

in your eyes on your lips again and when
you find yourself away gone into the new life
you did or did not imagine for yourself
how are you supposed to say that is who I am

that is where I am from when you've run away
into a world you do not even recognise
where dead dogs are thrown out with christmas trees
where the skies are orange and dusty wrecked

by thunder and tornadoes where the word home
makes you flinch and reminds you that all
runaways have the scar of failed attempts
like petty suicides on their lips

like a birthmark touched with a strange
curiosity where branches are swallowed
by the listening moon and flames are cupped
in hands here you spent yourself like a fever

to the house you once knew empty
derelict a body without belief where the walls
exhaled your name while you are perched
hunched wild-eyed before some small feast

of addiction like an angry owl pledging
your faith to the body body of the listening
moon still the two of us are running away
on a green cliff top in November

watching the waves wrinkle like birthmarks
in the night time rain through the muck
filled puddles with words skimming the water
of what we try to say like stones flung out

over the sea's expanse running
to the stray headlights of a mooring boat
down the driveway through the gate
into the laneway and the star-filled night.

The improbable flowers of Vizcaya

Outside, the fountains swallow the sun.
Again and again, I fall asleep
on Peacock Bridge
and dream of chasing kites

in my Italian childhood.
The living room replicates
a typical Renaissance room,
a high beamed ceiling,

a sixteenth century fireplace.
Plush coven.
Lumber room.
Loot.

The trees talk
in a prehistoric
gnarled and tangled
language. A two thousand

year old Roman tripod,
a fifteenth century Spanish
heraldic carpet.
Rococo ceilings

and two sixteenth century tapestries
depict the exploits of Hermes.
I want to sneak
into the butler's pantry.

No echo in my mouth.
Biscayne Bay, goodnight.
Beautiful Iseult, be with me
here,where the fishing boats

dawdle on the water
like small children
who should long have been asleep.
Here, we could walk

by the silk palm trees
with their gracious,
but improbable flowers.
You could say

you love me
and I would be Tristan
or whatever it is
you want me to be.

The Walk

after Chagall

I am a smear of lightning
over Barley harbour
briefly and writing to the sound
of rain is religion
my new blue singing religion
we took a walk
and grew too big for the town
we took a walk
over the hills the old fabric stitched hills
away from the town
out of the town the toy cornered town
it wasn't the wind
that took you into the sky
I held your hand
it wasn't the wind
I was happy or I was smiling
you flew like a kite
by my fingers and talked
about star apples
a fruit fallen from some far-off sky-past
a delicious edible pulpy mass
something to induce daytime visions

for days you wouldn't come down

On the avenue of the portal of angels #5

I didn't wake up
I was asleep all day
but still I arrived
a cloud with a treasure of rain
insisted

I saw the first snow drops of the year
in Forgney church
and promised to find some words
for the angel
who'd been following me

to feed the angel
I started with *snowdrop*
and suggested something from a life
I had led somewhere else
as a piece of parchment

onto which a phrase of gold chambered music
was inscribed
I became seasonal expectant
like one of those tiny pleasures
snowdrop

I know I need to contemplate
the vanishing moment
but this is not the time
when snow falls on snow
or one wave follows another

the angel's lips are drowsy
and I have promised
to feed it
with heavenbent dusks
and other pagan felicities

The Incredulity of St. Thomas

When he made love to a woman, the room is not important,
if there were a room, and the colour of her hair,
again unimportant, but red, that she was a stranger
may be of some consequence, in a town he had never before visited,

he looked into the woman's corn flower blue eyes, held her
firm beneath him and thought about the gravid night
when He appeared and bid him touch his wounds. He thought
about how his fingers had sought out the small cave

of flesh in the man's chest and how he had stumbled struck
with terror, how the calm sea of the soul was gone,
how waking dreams of snakes swallowing their own tails
followed him. What was wrong, she asked him.

He sat up, bemused, perhaps he looked out a window.
He might have seen an immensity of stars; he might
have sighed and thought how he could ask her whether
there were such things as forgiveness and redemption,

whether the night was but a veiled dream of desire,
whether his fingers had found anything other than longing.
He left the house, if it was a house, and the road was full of
        iridescent
dust, the heat made a tent of forgetting, the sun was falling

and he walked towards it, his mind opening like the unwalked
roads ahead of him. He did not ask himself whether the night
was the night or whether the woman standing in the doorway
was anything other than what it seemed, a twilight picture

with a moon hanging in the shape of a question mark,
but when after a time of walking he looked behind, he was not
surprised to find the town had already vanished, hidden behind
a cloud of dust or lost perhaps in the ravenous thicket of stars.

River of Light

red, green and yellow neon
blur the highway
into a river of light

the intersection appears
like a mirage
smoke wafting from the policemen's flares

call them mourning candles
three a.m.
surrounding the scene

the intersection
like a small island of sorrow
the car should not

be cut in half
so easily, so simply
but it is, there

we watch, dumb spectators,
held back
by yellow tape

as the police measure
confer and agree
the yellow plastic

covering the unnamed dead
flaps in the wind
like an ignominious flag

a warning, a reminder
flapping absurdly in rhythm
with the smashed blinker

of the halved car,
again yellow
until the ambulance appears

and departs, easily, simply
the shattered glass swept away
the car removed

the tape taken
so that everything
looks as it did

an hour before
when we passed
on the other side

an unending kaleidoscope
a blurring, ever-moving
river of light

To Dexter Above

i.m. Dexter Gordon

I picture you playing an old ballad
say *I guess I'll hang my tears out to dry*
in some god-awful after-life cellar
teaching the angels to swing, those patient
white-winged students waiting for the shabby
saxophone to start its praying, chipped
and dented, bedraggled gold like the sunlight
hazy, weak and sweet on those early
mornings in Paris, restless, unsleeping,
lost wanderings with junk and alcohol
beating through your blood, your eyes dark marbles
of loving suspicion, a face of ash,
itinerant fingers of exile, wry
shadow, old one time actor you paced
your way on grooves and glissandos full of
sound and fury, full of love and loss and
made beautiful burnished labyrinths
of sound, your gray lips, which you once dreamt bled
like the reed and your mouth and your lips all
blood, viscous velvet pain, wordless phrases,
expelling all the wonderful regrets
of our lives and when you make the horn talk
up there in your new home, in our night sky
the stars appear like startled orphans still
celebrating the wedding of brass and
wood, the luscious reed, how many thousands
did you lick and split in the blue frenzy
of hopeless dream-catching, in a sorry
attempt to conjure twilight, your inspired
improvisations opened like a long

letter to the night asking it to take
you and though our ideas of heaven may
be far too simplistic, because to bar
the blues from paradise would be nothing
less than blasphemy, the tenor of your
voice, gravel and dark, would not complain,
but blow the blue note and *Go* like an ever
enduring soul bark into the eternal night.

The heretic that makes the fire

What if this broken pale alabaster
had once been flesh, had once
felt the warm night air, and what
if these cold pursed lips were about
to say something, say, release a kiss,
and what if this bodice of cracked
stone were some kind of saint,
or like Hermione was about to speak,
what would it say, and what
you want to know, what kind
of person could have chiselled
such longing in stone, a longing
for god perhaps, or love,
though with the absence of two
clasped hands you wonder could
this hapless nomad of masonry
still believe in sin, for it is not
marble, nor gilded, but maybe it,
I mean you, can help, maybe if I
stay by your side and pray to you
before the sea takes you back,
maybe then I can be forgiven,
the way an unconvincing memory
is remembered, as if some parts
of us belonged to someone else,
forgiven for my own private
failures, not that I want to be
dipped in the River Lethe, but
what if this small feast of stone
could resuscitate itself and this is
the trick of the imagination,

albeit with a fever, and say to me
forgiven, but you won't, will
you, you will look dumbly at me,
you will say change your life,
you will leave me to wonder
if only time could slow down
and did not race away from us
and leave us confused at the day's
forays, leave us like sleepwalkers,
as I am now before you, kindling
your image like a heretic that makes the fire
and muses what wasteful war
brought you or were you thrown
from the armada by a mariner
priest, what ship went to ground
that you are washed up like this,
wet sand dousing your leg,
did you despair with the body,
are your lips chipped because
language could not articulate
your desire to be something
more, more permanent than
wasting flesh and what if you
are a sign, but that is what you are, isn't it?

The Straw Mannequin

after Goya

they think it funny
what they're doing to me
they laugh
they think it hilarious
hysterical creatures
my four sisters
my four wives
four women
I don't know
strangers they are
sirens if you like
how they found me
I don't know
look at them
made up like
a troop of tarts
dolls and as for what
they've done to me
tied me to a post
in McFadden's field
and filled my shirt
and pants with straw
took me home
after four days
without sleep
and painted me up
like a clown
I was weak
hallucinating
they took the sheet

off my bed
and carried my
weightless body
to the field
where they're throwing
me now up and
down like a
toy a plaything
a pet my neck
is limp out of joint
like a puppet's
my limbs jangling
like a set of soundless
keys my cheeks
are rouged and the sky
closes in and falls
away closes in
and falls away
I am weightless
and they laugh
and their laughter
arrests all other
sounds it fills
my head so I
can think of
nothing
of where I'd been
or who I was before
this charade began
or why I deserve
their derisive
hilarity
their shrill chortles
the four women's

strong as ox
flinging me
towards that lucent
crack in the sky
if only I could
make it to be
away from
their laughter
which fills my head
and the sky
and takes the voice
from every
winged thing

Ode to a Banjo

You need to wait for the silence
the silence snow commands.

You need to find yourself
obsessed and not with a woman.

I'm thinking of a soldier
from the Irish Brigade,

deserter, court-martialed,
listening on his last night

to a banjo with its bones
made of ghosts, poker faced,

goat-hide, wound, spell,
magic word, stamping

the gravely ground down,
a twisted ankle, from Donegal

to Down South.
There's something of the river

in the quiver of the strings,
cold on the feet as you step

in, and it's dusk or dawn
and the banjo with a moon for a head

is fading in the far off sky
where you are running,

your scent dispersing among the trees,
your childhood rising like smoke.

Far off you can hear it,
digging the soil, somewhere

in the forest, tempting
the scaffold with a body,

the snow's silence corrupted.
And the man who plays

the sodden tune, no one
calls him by his name.

In the Country Where it is Always Winter

after Pieter Breughel's 'Hunters in the Snow'

I am tired of romping in this cold beauty
in a land without memory where the wind and the snow ...
I am tired of the voluptuousness of winter.
This town is unfamiliar, not even as close as a cousin.

The sky is a dishevelled grey. The same pale colour
as my brothers' eyes. What they are thinking? I don't know.
We have longed since ceased to communicate.
What use? It does not stop our wanderings.

It does not help us to escape this country.
The country where it is always winter.
That these dogs are starving like the ragged souls of this town
does not surprise me. Did I say brothers?

At one time they were strangers, but when
that was I can't say. And the dogs too, vagabonds,
strangers themselves, immune to disease.
They follow us as if we had anything for them.

You'd think they would run to the fire, but
warmth of that kind is an illusion. What kind
of purgatory is it when the town's people skate on
ice? A town called temptation? If only we could stay here.

If only there were some kind of salvation in the snow.
The sound of the fire, dumb like the dreamless nights of sleep.
The children's voices I can hear, echoes in a well.
As for the swallows their immaculate twisting rends nothing.

And the dogs, the dogs, no whimpering for these mutts.
Just a slow sifting of the white ground.
Their anxious feet make the snow a poor betrayer
to the silence, a silence that rises like the dank

smell of smoke. A silence I have become used to.
Hoary and full of echoes. I want to say I left a loved one
          behind,
but I can't. Maybe I did, but I don't know now.
It's been so long. I imagine what she would have looked like.

But that again is another impossible task.
I can't get beyond the hands. A chilly alabaster, slender.
One last look onto the ice then.
Ice so hard I can almost dream of another life beyond its
          surface.

It carries our stern reflections as we descend.
Look, the trees stand with a wracked and solitary anguish.
They are like brittle black skeletons in the on-coming twilight.
And like windmills the children wave their innocent arms.

The Seducer's Diary

for Harry Clifton

As you were going backwards
Through the Brenner, I was coming out
The other side ... dawn, a field
Scarpered in mist. Copenhagen.
A train tumbling through the landscape of desire.

A man from Senegal mumbled
The Koran, as if to say the spirit
Wants to reproduce itself, to pro-create.
Yes, he should have married Regine.
Socrates had his shrew, Xanthippe.

I, too, was unprepared for the perpetual
Daylight of desire. The sardonic smile
Falls from his lips like a man jumping
From a cliff as the steps crumble behind him.
He does not shake his head, but holds it

In his hands. Regine for him was Schlegel.
'Will you never marry me?' Poor Regine.
The pseudonym will not save him,
Even if the diary helped him escape.
Think of lightning from a hill

In Budapest, if you like, where the ghost
Of Sandor might have walked. Wine
Cannot save you or churches or spires.
But, Harry, I do not think he walked away
From the flesh as easily as you imagine.

What nymphets, what spiritual flesh
Tempted him to teach her the erotic?
We cannot know. One prostitute was all
He had. His soul, a lantern wavering
In the darkness. His dilemma is ours.

The wanting spirit. Imagine he had
Taken a train to the body. Think
Of the lightning in his chest and the surprise
When he found himself stepping off
The train into another city, another life.

from the valley of dry bones

Berlin to Dublin, 1945

—sotto voce—

1.
A plush girandole spluttered above the rooftops. *Pray. Dream.*
Boots nuzzled the loose scree. *Dream again.* Luck. A lantern
swung anxiously. *On the ferry. You told me. To pray.* Where my
bones mumbled. *Dream. You are lucky.* About the winter.
Thank you. A dwarf poured his lament into the wind. *One of
the few. To be allowed.* While in the street a woman's eyes said:
Why. Thank you. I am going to open your graves and let you live.

2.
And the discarded wings of angels.

Tell me: there is nothing you need to know.
There is nothing you need to know.

A boat without oars jostles on the water.

Every time I want to tell you something,
what happened on my way here,
you say: take this like a bribe. Rain fell like fire burning.

Burns slow like green wood. A funeral. In a harbour.
Where swans.
Or like a glance at a clock that does not tell the time.
Like green wood burning.
Slowly. Never actually arriving. Like swans.
In a harbour. A funeral.

The words found like a horseshoe fallen
from the hoof of an old knackered horse.

Tell me: there is nothing you need to know.
There is nothing.

I have owed you this feeling since ... March.

This digging a hole. A small forgiving.

The words, a horseshoe hanging above the lintel.

There were nights when none of us spoke.
The speaking was all around us.

A tree. Money. The gutted night. A boat without oars.
Fingers crawling
across the country of the face. Fruit to catch.

Take this like a bribe. Rain fell like fire burning.
And angel figures. In a harbour.
Lanterns. Boots. A horseshoe. Like green wood.
Or a girandole.
Swans.

Your eyes so full of winter.

3.
your dizzy refuge a memory remade in rain
like the wind through the teeth of a swinging gate a river
in the rain swathed in rumour in unanchored light
a river or crabs crawling from their harbour walls
a city in mirrors the echo of people talking boots

a river through glass in a mirror in a river in a well
a frog a dead blue tit like wind or crabs in a harbour
people remade in rain echo the stars
you wore like rusted anchors into the sea

Looking for beauty in a crab pool

shiver water
skin of another
you have
so much to tell me
I know
I know
so much to tell me
shiver water
one crab
eating another

Sundays

First, you had to wear your Sunday best,
say a stiff navy blue shirt, ironed trousers,
slacks your father called them. Your shoes
you had to polish. You and your brother

bent over in the kitchenette, your mother
said *utility* room, rubbing the old yellow rag
over the football worn leather,
the laces you tried not to pull too tight

made brittle by winter's shrug. Next you would have
to find your father's keys, lost, misplaced,
hidden. A frantic escapade under cushions
and clocks where you stood about looking

in places twice, thinking already about the end
of mass, hoping he wouldn't catch you idling
and when the keys, sacrosanct themselves, were found
and you didn't have to help pour a kettle of steaming

water onto the frost inscribed windscreen of the car
you crowded into the back seat where the ascetic sting
of his after-shave waited with the thin lips
of his impatience. Your mother was giving it, mass,

a miss this week. Later, when you became an altar
boy, you were seduced by the language of faith:
the *sacristy*, a mysterious and alluring word you
relished like *tabernacle* or *liturgy*, cold on the tongue

like iron. *Chalice* had the reassuring inflection
of an austere dawn and all the authority and apparent
order that incited reverence like the chilling command
of a parent, as if the words were a punishment you

were thankful for. Men shuffled from foot to
foot at the back of the church like cattle
trying to shake the musty dank of their breed,
restless for the other public house to open.

The wind hustled its way
through the doors upsetting the tranquillity
of the candle flames where old women knelt.
You shuffled your way into the heavy oak pews

and sat and stood according to the priest's directions,
all the time looking at the girl in the seat in front of you,
her bare supple neck revealed as something
blessed and while St. Paul wrote to the Corinthians

you thought about devouring the flesh before you.
And then there hung poor Jesus on the cross alone.
When it came time to take communion
you mulled over whether to take it in your hand

or directly into the mouth and once you overcame
that one quandary you worried over how not to sink
your teeth into the body of Christ, something your brother
told you would send you straight to you know where.

It felt strange to have swallowed his body,
to have consumed the son of god,
to implicate yourself in something
which sounded like a crime, *transubstantiation.*

Outside the church after mass
your father gave you money, a pile of dirty coins,
to buy the newspapers and you waded home,
the headlines smearing your fingers with ink

and after dinner, maybe your grandparents were along,
before your father settled into his arm-chair,
you wondered briefly
what it was he might have prayed for,

whether he thought about Jesus alone on the cross,
whether he too was afraid of the dark
when the heavy oak doors of the church closed
and the candles, with a quiet gasp, were quenched.

Apologia

I wake to the sound of sirens
and stillness across the street
fire engines tumble away
to the fires of my imagining

if you look out the window
our neighbour Desiree
a name I've heard called out into the cold night
is being taken away

the first day we met her
her teeth sticking to each other
she told us we lived in the Galleria-ghetto
the poor among the rich

the previous tenant had been shot
dead in our front yard
nothing newsworthy not these days
I took the fridge she said without apology

but where will you go Desiree
now that you have no home
and where will red dog live
the birds argue about other matters

they turn the trees' leaves to a jubilee
and look the yellow lilacs are out of control
the pond I tried to dig in the back
a grave you called it is filled with water

the summer is on its way
you can smell it
welling up in the tough grass
another year tunnels its way to star-filled July

one of the cats you suspect is pregnant
frogs quake in road-side puddles
hundreds of them what am I to pray to
now that god has left me

the bar at the end of the street is sleeping
its neon in the morning looks dazed
I stop praying and start writing poems
apologias for not having lived a better life

notes to make me calm take stock
make lists and listen
closely to the interval between alarm bells
words to help me think about the car that passed

our house late last night and the shot
that was fired words to make me wonder
about that flare that golden hand
in the night and what it was reaching for

Seven Days in Chicago

DAY 1

On the first day
you said let there be pain
and there was

I've been whispering
the ghost of fires

drowning wake up
or let me into your dreaming
here my admission ticket

four charred fingers anything
burnt or broken a blue flame

how can I stop you from turning

I begin to burn

I'm not myself
I'm no one

I have to tell myself to stop wanting

the sky
to fall into your shoes

in the morning the wind
wants you

if it wasn't for people turning to stone

if it wasn't for dark bodies
or dilapidated hearts

DAY 2

I want to know
what the water is saying

retreating

I am jealous of you and the night
you're closer

the moon's in on it too

the trapdoor moon
you keep pushing me through

you cling to stolid Floridian palms

blindfold me

I've given you more than words

you want all the pain to be yours
but childishly I bruise
like the clouds at dusk

teach me how to love you
tell me how
you like to play Ophelia

I'm neither here nor there

busy with grief
like spiders in a pot
a wasp's nest

Day 3

I wait for any sign

the babbling voice not mine
the words not mine

talk to the night
persuade it to be something else

someone else

two green bananas
from the small tree
outside the house

I'm so hurt
I can't talk

did I learn this from you

the violence inside us

I sit under the sausage tree
waiting for the saxophones

to start their praying

you are there
slow eyed talker

two names pen-knifed
into that stodgy old oak

your face in the bronze water
my fingers paralysed
inchoate

a mess of light
this our blunt effort at love

Day 4

pale morning smells
honeysuckle eucalyptus

children in a playground
running like crazed ants

your dizzy life
making me sea-sick

goodmorning
to your soft pale skin
goodmorning

above your birthmark
your knee is bruised and swollen

I grow into the swelling
my fingers and my eyes

to be waking with you
the faint memory of you

I reach out of sleep
to be waking with you

from one dream into another
like opening a door

to the same room always
waking with you

the faint memory of you

DAY 5

let me guide you
come with you
now that I have no home

you come to bed
your clothes
lie
on the ground
without your body
where you left them
if you listen
to what we were dreaming
I am ready to rest

111

anywhere

red lake wind burning
coconut dragonfly
dancing over tadpoles
the shadow of a lizard
on scrap-metal

or the bells in Gründelwald

how can I hold you
with all your hurt
the desolate shaking

keeping us awake

I would have preferred a simple life
a life with simple things

Day 6

I am aching in your muscles
in the murmur of your body

if you find my soul
in the lost and found

taste it
slowly
the healing

that's what it said the insouciant wind

perhaps it was Tír na nÓg
this recurring dream
when Oisín fell from his horse

I think of Inis Mór
repeating to myself
that I wanted this silence
to empty the head

if it had not been for the week

or the blue songs
we could have been anywhere

but we were neither here nor there
we were busy with grief

like spiders in a pot

DAY 7

There was no seventh day.

Paris

after Celan

Make me bitter.
Count me among the almonds.
Drink
From my mouth.

Count me among the almonds.
The night is the night.
From my mouth
You almost would have lived.

The night is the night.
In the swell of wandering words.
You almost would have lived.
Without words too.

In the swell of wandering words.
You fill the urns and feed your heart.
Without words too.
Twelvemouthed.

And I lie with you, you in the refuse.
Get drunk and name yourself Paris.
Twelvemouthed.
As if we could be we without us.

Count me among the almonds.
Make me bitter.
You almost would have lived.
Make me bitter.

Oisín

a nightmare I drowned
a beehive was I in Spain
mills and oranges
an afterlife

I started to swallow
bones blind men
surrounded me
I was a boy with different coloured eyes

from somewhere originally
there were no faces
but numbers and months
a perpetual November of the soul

and here are your pockets
cul-de-sacs with stones
and old lovers so this is hell
a funeral again and again

the priest is turning the corner
turning the corner
dropping the chalice
they never played

the music you asked for
Liszt Hosanna
what's her name
men know about the soil

enough to fill their mouths with it
the country the city then hell
I never used to believe
my voice

was an echo in a well
never leaving my chest
I'm supposed to push
through this door

push through
I'm as afraid as when I was alive
I take a deep breath
I push through the door

I hear the bucket fall into the well

The Ring

We bought it in a pawn store
on Westheimer. We were already
married a year. You wanted
to wear it right away and not
wait on the charade I had planned.
You were right.
I wondered sometimes
whose ring it was before
it became ours, or yours,
how had it found its way
into the pawn store,
a small diamond,
among all the televisions,
video recorders, camcorders,
cameras, knives, jewellery,
pornography and guns.
Later, when it had all gone wrong,
when we had gone wrong,
when you had turned up without
the ring to take the furniture
that was yours, it was all yours,
I noticed the absence,
but said nothing. That night
I found the receipt
by the bedside table, no
note, just the ring's receipt
and I thought about it,
the ring, returned to where
it waited, to where it belonged.

Slowly Home

take the third train east
use no whips or spurs
but a gentle whisper
to encourage the driver

say good-bye to all you've known
but slowly, you have time
don't talk to your taxi
or pretend to be someone else

if the old guy takes you
on a detour, say nothing
smile politely, if you should
arrive in a strange land

where people no longer talk the tongue
you once knew, simply nod
and thank your fare
do not ask for directions

the stars obviously are not themselves
the headlines you suspect are a decoy
people leer at you conspiratorially
if you walk the streets

and you do not recognise them
no matter, if you happen
to stumble into a back-garden
weakly resembling a photograph

you once carried in your wallet
welcome the place with open arms
and the family that come now to greet you
take them, too, as your own

Leap Year Lake

at the asylum seekers support group meeting
where after three weeks the caring committee members
have still not come up with a name
for the party and have rankled over the words
for its mission with painstaking deliberation

I think of it, leap year lake,
the joy in just saying it, the lake
we passed on our way to Moydow,
after an afternoon of poetry in Virginia,
a palm of water which was not there,
hidden like an innuendo, or an unspoken
thought, curled up into some arid underground fist,

assumed though that it would arrive,
like a rumour
or a slur, the kind you hear on Dublin streets
about our guests, who are bored and crammed
and live under direct provision
which itself sounds like a sentence
to serve under

we are careful about what we say
in the constitution to the unnamed support
group for those who have arrived from other places
and may have names we can't pronounce and faces
we have not yet recognised

it's there as the politics and rhetoric
makes me dizzy an image of the lake arriving
like a black bead in a rosary of reds or blues

and the water, its water, the lake's,
leap year lake's water

is like a dark spell the sky has cast
its own secret reflection,
a beautiful disappearance elected to arise
once every four years, but by whom,
or by what, a common syntax or better yet
a language perhaps
which suggests sustenance, breath, life, our wish
to return always to where we started from,
to be present always, even when we are not
or cannot be

with the rain, which has created a season of itself
and which punctuates the lake's return
leap year lake
go on imagine you are there
by its banks now
pushing your memories out
like a boat
not with a name, an agenda,
but with an exhalation and a mysterious plangent
grammar, nominated, seconded, at once unanimous.

Ferry from Gotland

the crows are at my head again
a murder of them
wet and scrawny
milk and water
and dreams of gunpowder
flitting away another future

they haunt me
the ghost ships

a dream again
my life is made up of night time visions
a pier,
horses, flesh and blood and metal
carousing us into the water
and then onto an island
transformed

the footsteps, their echoes
are ours, again

night falls like the rain
again and again

darkening the way between our hearts

I thought my dreams would change

waves made of voices

too quickly the moment is gone

strange to see the medieval
revellers, teenagers in costume,
reliving something from so long ago —
their imitations are not even echoes

history is a party
invitation only

sounds to me like god-land
heaven's alibi

Maria, Maria

if you see a light in the distance
let it be me
coming towards you
a beacon
bringing you home

The Gate to Mulcahy's Farm

The gate to Mulcahy's farm is crooked,
sinking into infirm soil like a ship
from the Spanish Armada if you like,
forged and felled in some dark cave

to find itself jaded with flaking eroded gilt
leaving the striations prison-like,
shaded a coppery green. A gate without
a handle and unlike all others in any

neighbouring field without the dull sanguine
frame that swings to and fro like a hinge,
or a door itself to some other world.
No, this is no ordinary gate and there is

something majestic in its stolid refusal
to swing, something absurd even.
Perhaps this is another version of heaven,
imagine the bedroom it might once have graced,

this brass headboard, this discarded,
transported remnant of love's playground,
and look, two golden and intact globes
rest on either end, both transcendental transmitters,

receivers maybe of rough magic,
piebald love, communicating not sleep,
sleep no more, but wake, wake here
to the earth and imagine if you want

the journey of such an armature
of fecund passion, what hands gripped
these bars, what prayers were murmured
through the grate of this ribald cagery?

Imagine too the man who must have
hurled and pitched and stabbed
this frame into the ground, in a dark rain of course
after his wife had died, her passing to us unknown

though you know this
that there must have been some act
of violence within this frame-work,
some awful, regrettable pattern caught

in the form of what? Wind rushing through a brass
headboard, an exclamation point to the querulous
division of fields, could we be talking border-country,
and the broken, airy, moss-eaten stone walls.

Think about when the farmer died and the farm
was sold, think about what happened, the field, empty
of its cows, still with its stones and grey soil,
maybe this is Monaghan,

maybe some day it, the brass headboard
you are looking at now, will be sold
to an antiquarian in a Dublin shop,
brought there on a traveller's horse and cart,

not smelted down or disassembled, but sold
to a store where some lady with a wallet
will buy the thing, the elegant shabbery before you
that is the gate to Mulcahy's farm. As for the bed

itself, we can speculate, let it have sunken
into the earth, or better still let the earth be the bed,
the cot, mattress and berth to this sinking headboard,
this beautiful incongruous reliquary of misplaced passion.

from **The Orchid Keeper**

The Seals at Mill Bay, Rathlin

Dark black and brown and grey
dappled pelts soaking,
lazing and luxuriating in the sun,
still and stretching,
fatty sculptures, sea-made,
salt-nourished, below the disused
kelp store. Bladder-wrack
and long tangle drying in the sun.
A rusted anchor lodged
into the soil beside briny
black lobster pots. They lounge
and bathe and buoy themselves up
to watch, caretakers among
the throng of building.
The sun's light dispersing,
mottled on the water, shimmering
like the cobweb on the windowsill,
holding fast its thin frayed
filaments set shining below
a trinity of windmills. Barking,
majestic mythical creatures,

I imagine the lost diver among you,

his friends' masks and breathing apparatus,
fins and snorkels laid out,
their false skins discarded,
slung over the harbour railings
like so many seals,

The wreck he dived into empty,
the oxygen canisters empty,

among the black-eyed dreamers
his lungs empty,

but a seal's heart is full of love

which is perhaps what makes me
marvel at their watchful ways
and the perfect manner in which
they inhabit their bodies and dive
into the water that has carried
them to us and us to them.

Wintering

That was my last year in Florida,
illegal and thinking of marriage
as one way to stay. Sleepless nights
of argument and indecision. And

to keep us going I worked a cash job
at an orchid farm. Long hours
in the sun, poor in paradise, the heat
on my back, drilling for a living.

I worked with a Mexican.
My man Victor, the orchid keeper
called him, friendly and amused
at the affluent couples who came

to purchase the rich, ornate dreams.
We buried a dead owl together.
I remember that. And my body
aching in the sun. Floating home to arguments.

What we were doing I was told
was wintering. Getting ready
for the cold, its indiscretion, its disregard.
Nailing sheets of plastic onto a wooden

frame, hammering, drilling,
to protect the fragile flowers
and their steel interiors, their
engineered hearts and worth.

That is already a long time ago.
Its contradictions apparent.
Wintering in sunshine. The past
still growing towards the light.

I think of them now as some sort
of emblem of that past, ghostly
orchids shedding their petals,
as we winter here ourselves,

batten down the hatches and wait
for whatever storm is coming, whatever
calamity the cold has to offer us
in the same way the orchids do,

I suppose, waiting through winter
to emerge with budding, fantastical
and colourful insistence,
to wake and remind us:

be nothing less than amazed.

Ode to a Car Crash

part of the field
it breathes at night
moves a grassy beast
home of grub and worm

victory for wild things
a vision of the future
imagine the driver concussed
thrown from the vehicle

intoxicated bewildered
walking away from the site
the midden now
with a shake of the head

and a dismissive wave of the hand
years later the doors
are rusted unrecognizable
the wheels are gone

but the other driver
shadow driver ghost driver
some days in the night light
you'll find him still

clutching the steering wheel
as if he could take the vehicle
from danger at the crucial last moment
other days he's smoking a cigarette

invisible in the dusty sunshine
as a couple from the city
resettle into the countryside
circling his car's altar

he can never seem to leave it
he has the resigned look of the damned
not that he does not care
for his small cemetery

a caretaker a gardener of sorts
the soil grows the car sinks further
the ants make it home
a scrawny white cat hides from the rain

some days two teenagers kiss
in the back seat
the ghost driver watches shaking his head
what can he do

the boot is full of old clothes
but nothing goes to waste
one beggar who found the calamity
took himself a coat he still wears today

before long … what's in a lifetime
the engine is removed
transplanted to another vehicle
at least part of it

one which swerves its way
around corners in another county
the doors are taken
the seats removed

the glass is spread like fallow seed
its only contribution
to the growth
a glimmer and twitch of light

one day when the surviving driver
turns this bend again he shivers
the car he can't recognize
doesn't see it's submerged

the memory is faint was it here
what turns his blood cold
and pushes his foot
onto the accelerator

is the man standing like a negative
all light on the side of the road
as if he had been waiting
like an old friend

his arm outstretched
his thumb
pointing
all the way to eternity

The Surfers of Portstewart

before the sun sets its great crimson eye
drawing you to look upon its alchemical grace

the surfers of Portstewart take flight like some
mythical fleet gliding over the waves

which then cover them in ceremonial gloss
as they go down into the depths

to resurface an age away their heads
popping out of the water like eager seals

I watch them all day and all day I've talked
to no one but myself let's just say I stayed

not here but back where we started our trip
settled down if you like maybe I'd have met

someone lost as you would have it
lost to another life and no longer playing

the game which makes me wonder
what possible lives we could have had

can have remember the laughter
the monkey-business in the R&B bar

or the Akka tribesman plying his trade
who no matter what he held up for our inspection

a bracelet a scales to measure opium
lisped the word beautiful with such unique

and phonic idiosyncrasy beautiful
that everything from then on

was just that: beautiful like Yung
and the look of wonder and hopelessness

no I correct you helplessness in your eyes
when you looked at her something I'd never seen

in you before so Xian what does it mean
to live out our days among strangers

another world away I'm not making any plans
I don't know where I'll be come twelve months

but I wanted to tell you this:
all day I've talked to no one but myself

and watched the surfers of Portstewart
they are the magic in my day

with their devotional patience
sitting on their boards waiting

waiting for the right wave
the wave that will take them there

where they were going
where they were always going

the boy with the kite

three cars are parked on the beach
a dog is running to and from the shore

chasing the tide out and scampering
away as it returns lovers walk with lazy steps

a girl with ponytails dances with two
handfuls of sand but the boy with the kite

sees none of it not even the sea
blue and green and black and moving

his gaze is turned skyward where a kite
a flame moves like an ancient dancer

a soul on a string waving and flinching
and diving like a frantic seagull into the unknown

all day people have fished and surfed
walked and believed in all manner

of miracle cars ice cream the resurrection
of the body but for the boy with the kite

there is only one prayer he doesn't hear
the dog bark he doesn't see the dropping sun

or hear the sound of night like an alarm
bell ringing over and over he's a lone dancer

a devotee to the beauty of flight
an admirer to the ballet of aeronautics

he can keep it there the kite still
like a humming bird so you can't even see

its wings fluttering at speed he they the boy
with the kite the boy and the kite

are a poem in the making and when he
walks away in the sky above him

in its eternal blueness the kite pivots and burns

Fire of Stones

smooth to the touch
and dark like the eyes of a dead cat

did I say cat
I meant brother

smooth smooth
smooth enough to soothe

and clean a wound
almost

found in a fish
that lived after

you had cut
its gut and taken

those black jewels
from inside

found in water
cold and clean

deep water salt water
off the island

where nobody lives
but ghosts with warning voices

heavy stones small
stones seven stones

for wishing stones
to trust and heat

stones for your bidding
but not to be sold

hidden in soil
or pillows

wrecking stones
hell stones

gall stones
kidney stones

black night time
sold your soul stones

dream stones
rubbing stones

worried disappearing
finger stones

swallowed like the flames
they light

flint and bone stones
sharp enough to cut a man

like you

Ingredients for a Childhood Saturday

If you grit your teeth
and search for scrap wood
by the market, trounce

some wooden carts,
suffer splinters in the hands,
return home to find a saw,

rusted in the shed,
unused. Slide its flaked
old smile across a fist

of rock. Cut to
arms length. Two notches
at the bottom end,

three in front. Run back
through the market.
Stop, thump the dead discarded

pig's head. Load the black
rubber rings. Crouch down
by the river and wait.

Take aim and fire.
If you are quarry
to the gang next door

lay low, hide,
play dumb and for god's sake
say

nothing of your whereabouts
to the buddha of insomnia,
the owl, or his friend,

otherwise known as judas, the crow.

Lullaby, Dublin

the rivers are rising
I wish I were fluent
in the language you speak
but mine is a mouth

full of teeth a mouth full
of blood and broken teeth
a night without dreams
is like a life unlived

I imagine
snails clustered on a driftwood fence
a sticky orgy bud burst
besting unfolding horse-chestnuts

I woke reciting a poem
a dreampoem for you
waiting to be written
but the words washed away

like a shape in sand washed over
your face in my hands
or crabs crawling
from their harbour walls

someone is after you
you're running scared
through alleys
and out of the city

over rocks and water
how many times have you
had this dream of me
waking to the thought of your body

my words
are like bones buried
or breaking on hilltops
a fire in the distance

listen
rivers are rising
the night is slipping away
with buskers and tourists

pigeons radios rubbish
guards cold swans on the grand canal
portobello traffic double deckers
people walking late night

newsagents cheap red wine talk
wet silver birches shivering
traffic lights changing no traffic
empty roads regrets and prayers

the quays and conversations with the self
laughter phonecalls chipper
front shutters closing
onions in the wind

bedraggled priest with bunch of roses
secular misgivings bus
shelter smashed old walls
falling headlines in the gutter

parked cars dark houses
taxis speeding goodbye
closed doors song of the old
hoarse night harbour storms

gossip and suburban insomnia
romanian requests for coins
and a gentle rain and roads
the golden mosque and fires

lit in a field sirens voices
in the wind the body of christ
and pubs clapping closed eyes
fitful sleep and seagulls

rain falling a smile
yours a small kiss pressed
to the hands
like a gift

Towing an Iceberg to Belfast

for Rita Duffy

On the tip of her tongue

She's …

Don't think of melting

Pools along the way
A river

Think swimmers

Shipbuilding

On the long finger

She's …

Don't say it

Stop making sense

She's …

Towing an iceberg to Belfast

By a horse and cart

In wheelbarrows

A berg
A mountain
A mountain of ice

Read:

All poetry is performance
All poetry is L=A=N=G=U=A=G=E

Not the iceberg
An iceberg

Blue and ...

By dreams
With dreams
In dreams
Amen

She's ...

Towing an iceberg to Belfast

And gladly

To return

Return the scene of the crime
To its ...

She's ...

Towing an iceberg to Belfast

On the back
Of an old Morris Minor
An exploded artefact of sorts
From the Falls

We'll all be there
When she's coming 'round the mountain
Coming round
The mountain of ice
  The ice berg
    We'll all be there

Takes time
  And money
Poets with money
  Pleased to meet you

The latest craze
  It's the thing to do
It's what we wanted
  But never knew

It's like how come
  We never thought
Of this before
  It's real and imaginary

It's nothing like you
  Thought it would be
It's better than sliced fucking pan
  Or meals on wheels for that matter

It's not a trick
  It's no one starving themselves

For entertainment
       David Blaine meet Bobby Sands

Good night
       It's God honest
Let's have it now
       Straight and simple

And what of the ship
       What ship
Ghost ship
       Don't say its name

Swallowed by a bottle
Why not
Why not
A blue bottle
Buzz
And floating the waves

With a message
For everyone

Arrival time
Forever and some

Museum of ice
       Of found bodies
Returned to their resting place

Thirty years?
Agreed

Here she comes

Thank the ...
With the arrival of the iceberg
It is agreed
All poems are to be decommissioned

At last
The city
Exhales an icy breath

Ode to a Badger

us in a dirt mirror
a lurching likeness

bearded Hyde
keeps to himself

comes out late at night
hectic digger of sullen dreams

elder uncle
horatian headache

secret carnivore
has claws can kill

gnaws on bark
scared his face white

his laugh he lost
in his throat

little gorilla
with soot-saddened eyes

feasts on roots
and moonlight

there was always one
around the house

white-faced
black-striped

why you so moody
sniffed the sunrise

and swallowed the sun
badger baritone of loneliness

hoarse barker
tired of anything bright

angry dog
gorged on the whimsical

rabbit big weasel
coughing grumpster

querulous mole
big brother to the moon

nostalgic for blood and fever
shakes his head at ignited cats

once he heard the lark
now there is nothing

if you meet a dead relative
in one of these setts

sniff and move on
no point in mourning

king of charred hearts
and proud of it

crooked smiling minister
of the unrequited

sorry bear
closing your eyes to colour

clandestine neighbour
not unlike ourselves

when in fear
secretes repugnant scents

characteristic of the weasel family
brother to the skunk

Prayer

Once while waiting for a flight, I took
the underground tour of Seattle.
Starting inside Doc Maynard's Public House,
a restored 1890s saloon, the journey

took us through the subterranean city
and into the past where hollow street
sidewalks, old gas light fixtures and
wooden pipes crumbled with time.

Afterwards I sat in a café and drank
coffee. A mother and daughter
approached and asked could they sit
at the table. They introduced themselves.

Baptists from Texas. The daughter, a pretty
blonde girl, talked about her hopes
for marriage and disparaged her mother's
display of homophobia directed at our waiter.

She's old fashioned, she said.
The mother mumbled her own objections.
Before their food came, they held hands
and asked me to join them in saying

a prayer. My hands were taken by each
one of them and the mother prayed
aloud and thanked the Lord for the food
before us and my own safe journey.

When we had eaten, they drove me to the airport,
where I waited and thought about how
the mind has it own dark caverns and when
late at night I walk through them

to inspect their junk and clutter,
their beauty and sadness, I'm conscious
of the toll, something greater than Doc
Maynard's or the merchants who

carried on business in the lowest floors
of buildings that survived the great fire.
I think of the pedestrians who continued
to use the underground sidewalks

and of the homeless who gathered there,
those who gambled, smoked opium
or drank alcohol during prohibition times:
all banished now to the light and lurid world

where the blood still beats in America's
dark heart for me and for those who
take a stranger's hands in theirs and pray
with the certitude of the saved and forgiven.

my last poem

Longford, 2002

turn the television off
take the phone from its hook
light a candle
and close your eyes

what is it you wanted
what did you *long for*

you smile at the letters
writing them where you are

the missing 'd'
let it be for 'directive'

remind yourself who it is you wanted to be

a bedroom a reunion
Górecki's Symphony of Sadness
at least our bodies still know each other
the only words you recall

the 'd' the missing 'd'
let it be for 'desire'

who is it you used to be
who is it you've become
what is it you long for
what is it you desire

you're tired of being alone
of fighting with yourself
your heart you imagine
is a city
desire has made it old
its walls are falling
its bridges are on fire
there's a rumour of war

you long to be beloved
and for the right words
to keep you there
that is all

The Lady with the Coronet of Jasmine

I saw her again today.
Graceful in her poverty,
elegant. Her lips a luscious

sanguine escape. A bright
exit. Her tilted head,
diffident, but proud.

She passed me and I
smelt the fleshly odour
of temptation, heavy

in the air, eager to cling
to me. Her reckless smile
unhinging my composure.

But it cannot be.
It cannot.
It must be that my retirement

from public office is
making me drowsy,
like a summer bee

gorged on honey.
In actuality, it is twenty
years since I have seen her.

A man of my age
should not be given over to fancy,
to frenetic breaths

and tremblings. A man
of my age who at the start
of the century

heard the guns
from Edinburgh Castle
fire announcing

the abdication
of Napoleon and lived
to the end of the century,

I am ripe, and heard
his own voice,
by then a scant baritone

echo of what it once
had been, recorded by
the telephone, should not

indulge in flighty reminiscences.
And yet, memory trawls
my conscious thoughts back

to her, inevitably,
magnetically so.
And should I be so surprised?

A man, that is all I am,
a simple, imperfect man,
a man with a name of more portentousness

than pragmatism. William
Gladstone, a name, a gasp.
I say it to myself and it is

the name of a stranger.
I garden, try to remain calm.
I should make my peace.

But there she is.
In the soil as my fingers dig
for the flowers, there she is

haunting me from the past.
Emily Fenn was to be my saving
grace. An Irish peasant

from the wily shorn land
of Connemara in the West.
Wan refugee from the blighted

island next door. Alone, insomniac
walking the streets and keeping
company with other ladies

of the night.
I won't mince my words:
she was a prostitute

and I tried to save her, to rescue her
like so many other girls.
The grimy dirt of night fell around us.

Her voice was soft, plangent
like waves falling onto a shingled beach.
She mistook me for the wrong kind

of gentleman the first time I met her,
entreated me to the squalid
room she shared.

Her words were timid,
frail like chipped wood.
The misunderstanding over

we talked about her redemption.
I encouraged her to stay
at the House of Mercy

on Clewer and Rose Street in Soho.
But after a week she came back
and said she didn't want to be

locked away, that she would
have committed suicide had she stayed.
I calmed her, sat her down.

We entertained long conversations.
I read her Tennyson, which she confessed
to being much impressed by. Indeed

her very shape seemed to waver
in the candle flame, and so great
was her sincerity and enthusiasm

in this regard that I actually
gave her my signed copy of *Idylls*
and within a week she had memorised

large sections of it.
Another day.
It is no good: the calendar is

wearing me away and I can think
of nothing else, but her.
I confess, I went out of duty,

but also out of need.
Light falling on her hands,
elegant and white. My desires grew.

I sought her out. The desire
I felt when I walked the shoddy streets
of London was calamitous.

It seethed in me;
it burned, raged, galloped, slammed,
transported me into all manner

of reverie. Woman. I wanted to enter,
possess, raze and rebuild your
mysterious form, to enter

your hypnotic realm.
Emily, you represented to me
all the beautiful possibilities

of life and I courted evil
only to overcome it. I went
to her again and again and

because of the hardships she
had endured and the tales of hunger
and desperation she told of her native land,

to say hardship would be an injustice,
it was misery what she described
and all the more so for the unpleading manner

in which she relayed the story of her life,
as if such privation was itself
what God had deemed her and her own

worthy of. Six brothers, three sisters.
Her mother dead. I can hear her voice.
I am happier here, she'd say.

Though, I don't feel like the same person.
I feel like a completely different person.
And eventually I would leave after talking

for so long with the grubby feeling of money
in my hands. My garden does not need
my tending. I sit. Foolishly, I read.

My mind is moidered.
The words on the page are a weak echo
of the literature I once read.

Books with impure passages,
concealed beneath the veil
of a quite foreign medium,

so I drank the poison, sinfully
because understanding was thus hidden
by a cloud—I have stained my memory

and my soul—which may it please God
to cleanse me, as I have need.
I have read sinfully, although with disgust,

under the pretext of hunting
soberly for what was innocent.
And though today, I read the good book,

Corinthians 10, I am still afflicted
with too many memories.
I read, 'No temptation has seized you

except what is common to man.
And God is faithful; he will not let you
be tempted beyond what you can bear.

But when you are tempted,
he will also provide a way out
so that you can stand up under it.'

But Lord, this is more than I can bear.
Where are you? Answer my prayers.
When I walk those streets again,

admittedly a good deal slower,
I see her. I know it is not her,
but some likeness, some young fresh face

with a halo of jasmine. My mind
is playing tricks. And for a moment
I am happy. I think of the day

she sat for the painting my friend Dyce
composed of her, how he made her
immortal, pure, clean, after

my avaricious attacks of desire.
She was angelic, fine, the fond
glow from her cheeks forgiving me

and when he asked me to place
on her the coronet of jasmine,
I felt all the humility of a disciple.

The incredulity of Saint Thomas
with his fingers seeking out
the cave of flesh in His chest.

Yes. And yet, I suppose I felt
the guilt of Pontius Pilate.
But what grace the painting lent me.

For in it, she is gazing at me,
the missing subject, the beloved.
This is the chief burden

of my soul, rending it
to a ragged status. Desire
is gone. Mnemosyne

has chosen her to be my muse.
My wife Catherine is here,
all my loved ones. And yet...

And yet I remember returning home
time and time again to scourge myself.
The skin on my back blistered and bled

like a map of my misdeeds.
I did not tend to those wounds.
My penance was pain, physical,

self-inflicted, hopeless pain.
Even today I went to find her.
But of course, she was not there.

Only the weak resemblances I am
afraid to converse with.
And if I could find her what would I say?

Our friendship lasted but a year,
before she made her way to America.
Of course, I should have written.

She is surely living a powerful life.
How can I depart this stage
with no fond thought of those around me,

only the desperate recollections
of a short wild passion?
Coded diaries. And yet,

I think I loved her. What awful
headaches I've had today.
I go about my chores with the lethargy

of the old. I sit in the dark
to quell the pain in my head.
And now I have oral hallucinations

to contend with too. My loved ones
turn around me and weep
as if my condition is something

they can do anything about.
The redemption of these poor creatures,
that's what I wanted, now it is my own

salvation that is necessary.
I have set down a black mark
against this day, like so many others.

Give me penance, O Lord, worthy of my sins.
Tomorrow is Sunday.
What kind of atonement can He conjure?

Will He take this emblazoned image
from my mind? As if the woman
with the coronet of jasmine was a curse.

What penance will You find for me?
How will I move from this purgatorial
conflagration? And, Lord God, do I deserve to?

Map Lover

for Aoife

you will gaze
at a map on a wall
a map of intersecting streets

of a city
you have or have not
visited that may or may not

exist
you will gaze
inspect and study fondly

the oldest
and rarest of maps
of Dublin too your city

for hours
and with the same
concentration you lavish on

your music
or me because you
will look to my eyes and hands

to my lips
my body your fingers
tapping out a cadenza onto my spine

as if I too
were a map to
the conversation of our bodies

and then
bless you you will
with all the consummation

of a map lover
always and forever
find your way to me

Variation on the word 'love'

In these dreams
I always used to be an observer
but now things are happening
and I'm part of it

one of my friends dies in a parachute
in the ice

and there is a horse with rooms
cold medical rooms
a secret corridor

I'm scared sometimes
of the unexplored caverns of the mind
its otherworldliness
its strange calendar of back to where
you've never been
its dream logic

I would like to love you
in another time
say Berlin 1923
when Brecht is prowling under the lindens

I would like to love you
which may not happen
I would like to make love to you

but the dream is like a film
made up of shots discarded
on the cutting room floor

I wonder what people mean
when they say silence
what comes with it
must also mean the end of voices

today it is snowing
and the afternoon is bruising nicely

I have decided the following:
Berlin is a good idea
1923 or no
life may be but a dream
but love is a dream
that silence and snow are one and the same
especially if you find yourself
lying in a field and someone
is calling out your name
and it's snowing
but it's not your name
and something in the wind
as it makes its way through the grass
you are lost in
finds you
so that when you stand with your head
finally empty
you'll recognise the clouds
and the landscape they shadow

from **108 Moons**

Half-open Windows

Spring-time
music is playing
through half-open windows
somewhere in the distance
I remember
its whiff
from childhood
saxophone sound splinters
cut veins
in adolescence
a desire for love gushing
later nostalgic
tunes flowed
with the remorse
of self-betrayal
now it comes back
like a salty longing
for a lost
Promised Land

older now
I already know
nothing will change

I will be a child
again.

Pain

Pain comes
with a bouquet of irises.
Why irises?
I don't know, but they are
dark purple –
that's the way it hurts.
Maybe the shapes of leaves
are to blame —
they are well sharpened
kitchen knives,
fine double-bladed daggers,
dangerous iron-ore scythes;
wounds are deep
festering, long-healing.
Pain's fingers
are thin and blue,
when they pinch
lumps and bruising appear.
Pain grips me, holds tight
and doesn't let go,
smiles an orange smile,
flashes yellow
owlish goggles in the dark.
A black topper
cocked on top of the head,
a sweaty forehead,
a coattail that hasn't been cleaned for a long time
you can say no more
of a dirty, un-ironed shirt.
Every night we play
he loves me — he loves me not

however hideous he might be
we start at twelve sharp
and continue until morning:
painkillers do not work,
sleeping pills do not help.

There

It is good There where we are not
fish have tongues There
and give French kisses,
birds don't fly There,
but play the piano —
Chopin, Beethoven or Yesterday,
centipedes sit on hallucinogenic mushrooms
and smoke pipes There,
people are madly glad There
and greedily pluck each day,
the days are rank There,
only the nights thrive with the weeds.

On the Plane

Those sitting by
the emergency exit
should abandon everything
but hope.
No doubt no doubt
handbags and briefcases
will hinder a headlong fall
from the dropping liner.
Wraps, throws, or cloaks
are not needed either,
hungry interspatial spirits
might get caught in them.
The beards of poets
are less than desirable,
first of all
the devil might grab them.
It is advisable to shave
even leg hairs,
when erect they become sharp
and might tear the clouds.
It is necessary to
take off all your clothes
be naked as newborns,
lovers or corpses.
At crucial moments
nudity is unavoidable —
as in Bosch's *Paradise and Hell*
or in Memling's *Last Judgment*.
Once fallen everyone
will swarm
with ruthless smiles
between the propeller blades.

Breakfast in a Hotel

Bodies with their sleep-shroud
uncovered
drift slowly
into a breakfast-purgatory.
Eyelids swollen with heavy sleep
don't let anything through –
a minty aroma hides the foul smell
of decay coming from mouths.
An incongruous death dance starts
around the sarcophagus of the table
decorated with golden cheese leaves
and a pink ham mosaic.
Gravestone toast squares
the blind eyes of hard boiled eggs
the yellow bile of yolks
and the quivering brain of jelly.
Fat sausage fingers
point prophetically towards heaven
artificial honey is dripping slowly
like tenuous time.
Knives and forks are beating the rhythm
of warmed plates, but
the lead heaviness of dreams
stiffens the dancers' steps.
To have breakfast while everyone's watching
is shameful — it's like undressing
in the middle of the street and being molested
by a passersby.
Suddenly
the unbearable tension explodes
with the scream of a falling teaspoon.
Help yourselves.

Nowhere

Nowhere is not a place,
but a gap between two words,
a space between heartbeats,
a short blink when
the eyelashes meet.
Nowhere doesn't start and doesn't finish,
it has no determination,
doesn't give in to definitions,
but buzzes at the ear
like a giant bee, bigger
than a thousand galaxies.
I fall into nowhere when
I desire sweetly to disappear
or when strangled
by spring beauty
more bitterly than bitterness
I am afraid to die.

Things in Themselves

When I am not at home,
things have orgies,
get horribly drunk,
sin with each other,
change their
usual shapes,
turn into emptiness,
but as soon as I
step inside, they turn back
into themselves again,
freeze
and pretend
to be dead,
they are silent
when I talk to them,
they don't open up
to a caress,
they become riddles, mysteries,
as great as Yahweh,
and ask unanswerable questions:
why is a chair a chair,
why does a table need four legs,
who made a bed be a bed?
Only a china cup
suddenly caught
at the crime scene,
jumps from the shelf
and falls to pieces.
It's a pity,
it was a good thing.

Blue Sparks

I live as if swinging
on the tongue of a bell
sometimes hating myself loudly
sometimes loving myself quietly

*

108 moons stiffen in a rosary
fallen stars stick in the snow
on a dazzled night at the foot of Kailash
time is not passing not passing not passing not passing
not passing

*

I often wake up rooted
in the middle of an endless circle
I can feel the horror
there is no place to go

*

I bow to my Lama
an old woman with the face of a maiden
who turns passion and sorrow
into a drink of immortality
for dakinis to taste

*

Lulled by passing
joyful and sad days
I'm writing my songs
on stones

*

A spinster rejected by all men
a most desired lover
a monster from the cemetery
a beauty with a skull-drum
a friend of death
a demon-tamer
a mad nurse to those who have lost hope
a virgin consoling the sick
a whore dreaming about a horse-like penis
the most faithful wife of the Lhasa monk
a three-eyed goddess with a ferocious smile
these are my shapes which I change
whenever I feel like it

*

Roadside taverns
are swarming with drunk men
pouring praises
onto the mad yogini

*

I run in water
without getting wet
sink to my knees and turn to stone
I don't burn when hit by lightning
just fall to pieces from longing

*

This perfect body
is full of passion hope and fear
but they are only illusions
I create and destroy

*

Routine everyday actions
are falling like syllables
meaningless mantras
won't bring Enlightenment

*

I stab my eyes and can see
Samsara — Nirvana's ornament
a string of precious
stones and shit

*

The day's reddish bud
opens in the afternoon
and shrinks in the evening
I cover myself with its withering petals

*

The day is fading
night is coming
in the hour of dusk
the silent world

is changing
I overstep my limits

*

The morning is hiding
dreams are chased away
I climb to the top of my insomnia
red clouds of dawn
are hiding the temptation to disappear

*

In the early spring morning
while darkness still lingers
a lonely bird starts to sing
the veil of illusion falls away

*

Like the invisible walls of illusion
I can't overcome
I can smell freedom
the way an animal can smell water
in the middle of a desert

*

The old doctor sinks
his fingers into the winds of my body
counts the remaining days
steals half my life
shrinks back and flees

*

While drowning or being drowned
my desire for one gulp of air
is stronger than the sacred doctrine

*

Cursed and chased by an honorable Lama
soaked by rain whipped by hail
I am shouting and dancing
in the middle of the desert
blue sparks flying from my bare feet

City of Gods

The smoke of incense
is spreading lazily
into the turquoise sky
of the city of gods
morning salesmen
are shouting: milk! milk!
bread! bread!
on a white side-street
I find comfort
in a small piece of iron

*

The inhabitants of the holy city
are eating labouring excreting
sleeping praying making love

and skeletons are dancing wildly
in the fair of confusion

*

In a cemetery near Lhasa
a she-wolf with empty nipples
is trying to find comfort within me
I can smell the autumn

*

When I return to Lhasa
after three long years
without even bowing to the gods
I start looking for myself

188

*

Your greedy hands
your irritating fingers
are stuck between my ribs
too close to my heart

*

You promise me peace
it scratches at me painfully

every night I collect my flayed skins
from the dirt floor

*

Surreptitious glances
while praying to *Allseeing*
burning touches
while worshipping *Thousandhand*
in a crowd
little black stones
won't build a bridge
between me and the one not destined for me
not even after we have crossed the valley of Death

*

The way a poor magician
is hurt by the tricks of his own creation
I bend with pain
the moment I remember you

*

When I meditate
skies flow into me
I embrace the earth
and melt in ecstasy
but you are not here

*

I am a madwoman —
sleeping in cemeteries
eating leftovers
wearing what is thrown away

in my sad heart I am carrying
the forbidden face
of the Lhasa monk

*

When I am sworn to love
I cannot answer
because all the wealth
I had gathered in my heart
I have given to the Lhasa monk
who has broken his vows

*

Armfuls of withered yellow chrysanthemums
are thrown into the fire
in an empty monastery yard
when the summer of longing is over

*

In hours months years
I will remember your caress
nervous and hot
erasing time
running out
through boundless space
freezing in eternity

*

When I reach the peak of despair
I take love's worn-out rosary
and string memory's beads onto it
with long fingers of sadness

*

Gods put on masks
sit down into the lotus of my body-mandala
and start talking
in voices which are not theirs

*

Butchers' laughter
and lambs' blood
soak into the first snow

I am leaving Lhasa

Glass Mountain

White Mount Kailash
Egg of the Universe
I fall to your feet
I am the one obsessed by lust

*

At the roadside you pick up a flower
a horse-mare
you place its blue petals in an indecent manner
and say: as a child
this is how I imagined
adult love to be

*

On the night of the full moon
on the way to Tingri
the messenger
who passed me
cast no shadow

*

In the fog at sunrise
a yak shepherd said to me:
darling if you are looking for enemies
your wish
is an order for everyone

*

In a blue mountain cup
on New Year's morning
while warming hands by the fire
the wine of the sky is bubbling

*

I am climbing and climbing
then stop to catch my breath
a Kailash yogi whispers to me:
I envy the mountain
that makes you breathe
with such passion

*

All boundaries overflow
milk and blood start boiling
a man as pale as the moon
breathes out my life

*

An old Master
asks me to sing about my favourite mountain
he interrupts me:
your love will not be answered

from **The Last Falcon and Small Ordinance**

Promise

You get off the train
in another no-where town
and are welcomed home.

The wind leads you
to a road and you start
to walk.

Where you came from
is no where like this.

A man is pushing
a bike. He tells you
the rain is on its way,
but you don't see.

He offers you
a place to sleep.

You keep going
to where there are fields.

Not far from a river,
someone is calling out.

A woman is standing in
the doorway of a house.
She sees through you.

In her silence,
there is something
of a promise,

something
which suggests
you could
if you wanted
become again
the person
you wished to be.

You can hear the voices
of children,
their laughter.
You can choose to walk on.

You've been travelling
a long time.

Before you speak
the first words of the day
you can rest.

The world is waking.
And the morning is welling onto your lips.

Speak.
Say something.
You can still be healed.

To the Future

in the morning you are woken
by the engine of loneliness
you have lived such a short time
you have lived such a long time

each day stretches out
like the barrel of a gun
lovers die everyday
and the ennui of sirens and alarms

makes you nostalgic
for Vera Lynn's 'Harbour Lights'
or the black and white's
on Sunday afternoons

highways and hotels
and the new neon crucifix
keep the city what it is
and still where else would you be

not Tangiers
death has a new army
but we still need to love one another
or get through today anyway

the future is already here
and even if the cars are crashing
and the money's tight
someone says I love you

and someone else means it
there'll be new gods
to curse and disbelieve
new sports and books to read

if you listen carefully
the letters and stories
are already gathering
like a group intent

on demonstrating
something like solidarity
illicitly or not
they may be our only hope

Dawn Sun

if people had smuggled animals
onto the bus I hadn't noticed
the fields were silver in the dawn
church goers wrapped themselves in their myths
and out of the earth the old cries came
no one noticed heeded or believed
nor in the road's plaintive appeal

so be it ... the dead lined the way
waving farewell or ...
hats were doffed smiles no not smiles ...
workers stood up from the fields
and watched our passing
some with envy some with regret
the smell of schnapps was something we shared
there were no songs but heavy sleep
pale eyes expelled smoke

and the dawn sun startled us with its cold fire
my words had already banished me
but I hoped our bodies might meet
before the scrap-yard of longing
closed its bloody gates

I was unsure in the new city
tripping over memory's shoelaces
when the light of mid-morning
warmed my feet
and I danced over the river

you were surprised by my voice
calling out to you

on the street
but you should not have been
that is what it had been doing
for a long time
since the time we first met
and before

The Last Falcon and Small Ordinance

No one was there when I returned, not a soul
though each one of the settler's personal effects remained:
some wrapped in dust, some overgrown with grass.
Axe, file, compass. Scuppet, dice and pipe.

Iron pots rusted. Maps and books spoiled by rain.
Words sank into the soil never to be heard again:
words like *love* and *peace*. In this moon-shaken dawn
there was no evidence of a struggle, no sign of violence.

On a tree in Roman letters *CRO* was carved and so I ventured
toward the point of the creek, but again found no sign
of the settlers, nor of the last falcon and small ordinance
I had left them with. The colony was lost; it had disappeared.

The maps of the New World were to be my task, but
there would linger about this place a shadow,
one which no cartographer could draw and the name
Roanoke became the ghost of a name. What then

must have happened remains but a mystery.
Was it a massacre or an assimilation of sorts?
In these my last years, I have often wondered
while making maps of land for Raleigh's tenants in Kylemore.

I have wondered and dreamt, dreamt and wondered.
But nothing, no answer nor salve has come to me,
no visitation of grace either, whether I have prayed or not.
I have lived since then a quiet life. I know my granddaughter

to be the first English child born to the land, a fact
which should make me proud; but it does not.

Instead I'm left with a feeling not unlike guilt,
albeit a guilt tinged with something like awe and regret,

a feeling of being alone under the old world's white skies.
And even if my memory fails me, even if the voices
fade, I can still see ingots at the bottom of the sea
and hedgerows on fire. I see too how history cannot map

whatever losses the heart has held and I hear cries
for help in the forest or rather an echo thereof,
and within the undulations of this wild landscape
I fear it simply to be the wind exclaiming

or my own faltering mind telling me something
it ought not to have forgotten, a clue perhaps to what
may have happened, but the words, whatever words there were,
are still too feint to make out, still too distant to hear.

A River in the Irish Midlands

the stones shine like silver
and sink into your hands
slip into knots and become
the anchor of a longing
that will not break its bounds

where water is alive with voices
and sunlight wickers and shakes
the fronds and gold flowers
rain's witness calls out a clue
to the secret of the river

and a girl's drowned eyes
extinguished sometime blue
ripple and rise into the net
of an anyday Sunday memory
what they say is simple:

no one fishes here anymore

Zero Point

I closed my eyes
And told you what I saw
You said no
But I kept on

The garden showered in light
The eucalyptus towering and diving
And waking us with its myths
Its stories of my grandfather in Spain

At war his poetry and how he took
When he returned to Ireland
His life and the life of the one he loved
And in broad daylight

Imagine the family's shame
Which is why I am writing in the dark
And why you are wondering
About the zero-point of our love

I don't blame you
Well maybe a little
Another reason I keep talking
As though I had a theory of everything

And why you think to live for ever
No great shakes
Too many full moons you say
Is that I've often wondered

About what will be in the long to come
That is when at night my lungs
Aren't filling with water
Nearly wrote eyes instead of lungs

And before I forget
Today I saw a hungry blackbird
It's cold you know
Colder than a coal miner's face

Rubbed its orange beak
Into my hand
Felt like the time
You put your hand

On the tensile fence
On the farm of your childhood
Or your grandmother's
My merula to your moses

Amen
How this turned into a memory
Of you I can't say
And all of a sudden

My date palm
My caucasian chalk circle
I your gentile
Your barbarian

I imagine we meet
In one or another future
Where it happens again
On an old road

I throw stones
At your glasshouse
Take the shards from your hands
And let the bird fly

Visiting Hours

I am driving northwards across the border
into south Down and farther north, driving
through a lean vegetation into summer,
golden and sweet, allowing my mind to wander

to familiar and unfamiliar places. A map
lies on the passenger seat beside me.
I've reached for it, but am distracted
by the ten white crosses on the embankment

before Newry which makes me think
of you and your troubled time: how
you'd hid beneath the bedclothes,
a starched white sheet and old blue blanket,

one which reminds me of our childhood.
'How do I know it's you?' you'd said
from under the dishevelled canopy you had created.
'How do I know you are not just a voice in my head?'

I've tapped you on the back to stir you
from your week-long disturbances, shifting
from sleep to waking dream. You groan
and move and peek out at me from under the covers.

Chocolate bar wrappers and sweet packets
litter the bed-side table. Bottles of water and
juice stand half finished. You sit up, finally,
not with the mock machine gun you fired

the first time I went to visit you.
'It could happen,' you bellowed dispensing
several rounds at the other patients.
This time your one caveat is:

It's worse than one flew over the cuckoos nest.
Said without the grin, but with the doleful
look you carry on occasion, the same no doubt
when you met in Spain two men from the IRA,

two men you say, who followed you there
after three years surveillance to interrogate
and torture you. I had just started to work
on the border when you fell into your troubled

state, filling out funding applications for peace
and reconciliation. 'Peace money,' is what
they called it, as if such an ambition had a price tag.
I wondered now as I drove across borders

what solicitude it would take to bring you back
to who you were. Not, I imagined, a doctor
who asked me if I thought what you talked
about had happened, had really happened. This

is your story, but I know you're not going to tell
it, not again, not with the relish and obsession
you did while still in it.. Your time
inside was frightening, but amusing too.

When you were called for dinner once
and I went to leave, you pointed to a bed
and told me I was welcome. The next day
you recounted how the paramilitaries

had administered pain killers. Truth drugs,
you called them. You talked about how
they kept you against your will, how they
tried to drown you. I turn the radio on,

but it serves no distraction and so I drive,
drive on with the thought that this then is the legacy
of the conflict, or one of its legacies.
That after the bombings, the shootings, the warfare

and ceasefires, after peace and reconciliation,
what we, what some of us, are left with
is a man in a hospital bed, afraid for his life.
Drive on. And I do, into unknown territory,

marked with flags, unlike the mind
which is an unmarked maze, past Ballymena,
towards Coleraine, past the bunting
and the painted curb-stones towards

the end of another journey,
the end of another reverie and what I am
left with is the same uneasy satisfaction
I feel when leaving you on those occasions

after visiting hours are over, namely
the questions: what is real, what happened,
what really happened? And dear brother,
part of living, part of the struggle, our struggle,

I suppose, is that no matter how much we think
about it, interrogate our pasts or actions,
no matter how much we beseech you
or each other, we'll never really know.

To the Book of Kells

He woke after what seemed
like a hundred years of sleep,
found his clothes, recently
returned to him, walked down

the stairs and out into the daylight.
He walked slowly. It felt
like he was walking on the moon.
His feet rose and wavered,

floated, he sprang from one foot
to the other. Everything
sped by him. Cars, people,
and dreams. His own thoughts

remained deliberate, careful.
Past the brewery, down by the river
shining in sunlight, he walked.
When he reached the Book in its tower

he gazed at its arcane colours
and curlicues and heard the vellum
like wind through a field soughing
and shifting. He thought if the island

Iona and the visions of the monks and
then of his own recent and strange
imaginings. Fantastical paranoia.
IRA plots, accusations, kidnappings

and tortures. After swimming
in the sea of the Book, he shook
himself dry and walked slowly
along the river, dark now, but still

with hints of gold and green.
No one noticed when he returned
or that he had been gone
in the first place. He went to the bathroom,

removed his clothes, took his robe
and went back to bed. It was not
night, but he closed his eyes anyway
and entered not darkness but

another world where the Book began
to grow, gain strength, and as he fell
into a fitful sleep, to thread and stitch
its way tightly and colourfully into his dreams.

Only at Night

the calendar flies from its stoop
like a frightened crow

and the days fall from each other
only at night do the hours grow

seem longer
allow you the chance to breath

dusk lends you time
and history's ashes are whistling

in the air
in the wind

in the ...
you name it

no more honey
in the hives then

you'll not outstare the lightning
only at night

can you think and when you do
the mirrors shut their doors

and your life a maze
presents itself with only one way out

what you're left with is
desire

sometimes there's nothing (left)
to praise
but the darkness

On the Way to Three Rock

What it was that lead me
through the fields and into forest
I can't say, but whatever it was
it felt like a compulsion;

in other words, I had no choice
in the matter. This may have
happened before, but somewhere else.
In the forest there was the dense

smell of pine, underfoot the crunch
of kindle and out of it like smoke
rising from a dead fire
came the fluttering of birds and

their voices above me in the trees.
Suddenly I was there in the clearing,
high up, watching a boy pitch a tent
and a girl watch him. They fumbled

together in the dark, they held
each other like first-time lovers.
They did not see me; I was not
to be seen. Besides what would

I have said to myself: that the mist
in the morning will be cold and
the moon, it will stay
hanging in the sky at least until dawn?

Winter

Winter arrives secretly,
puts a chill into your dreams
you hardly notice, makes
you shake and think

of somewhere else.
The leaves fall
from the trees,
they say something to you like

leave, get out while you can.
Before children arrive,
before chaos comes
before the forgetting of what you

wanted to do with yourself,
once upon a time, dawns.
A friend calls,
says lets hit the town,

get outta here, go drink,
meet women,
leave it all behind.
It's not even someone you know.

You go gambling.
You lose. You forget where
you parked the car.
You hitch

and wake up somewhere
where it's summer.
It's what you wanted.
The girl beside you

speaks another language and
slowly you begin to understand.
It's about unpaid bills
and outstanding debts.

It's nothing to do
with living for the now,
whatever that is.
You roll over onto your side

but before you do
you catch a glimpse
of her dissatisfaction:
it's in her eyes,

they have something
of winter about them.
They put a chill
into your dreams.

They make you think
of somewhere else.
Instead of running
you tell her yes

you will put the trash out,
but not now, please not now.

Tender Accomplice

I walk towards the sound
it is at first indecipherable
inscrutable
gradually it becomes clearer
the sound of voices
the sound of people I know
and do not know

perceptibly the sound rises
like the wind on the lake
it picks up and darkens my vision
it dizzies the forest
and covers the pathway
it turns the world into a storm
and I turn and turn again

I turn to walk
from the sound
I turn to silence
tender accomplice
which is nowhere
and falls slowly and darkly
like a late snow

Kite String

when he put
the gun
to my head

I thought
of a childhood
summer

in Wicklow
I felt the
wind

tug
at the kite
string

in my hand
I saw
the blood

stained
wool
on the barb

and the
chicken eggs
warm

and
soft
in my hands

I felt them
too
once more

Prophecy

after Sandor Csoori

the last winter will arrive
with the sound of bells

and wheels covering cobblestones
horses too will neigh and whinny

from their tar-black nostrils
eternity will pour its lullaby

men and women will declaim
of their innocence

and sink into the shadows
children will take to the streets

fire will arrive
light the lakes and water

no god will condemn
no god will forgive

but people will burn
all day and all night

and there will be
no resurrection

Whatever

Back then you were full of impetuous
passion, all or nothing promises,
like the hot Mediterranean sun in July.
Said things like now or never.

Words were like drums.
And you climbed all the trees.
Painted your face
and tried to fly a thousand times.

Clover and honeysuckle
you tangled in and drank.
Chickadees chirped for you
and the nights conspired.

Somewhere in the haze,
the drop-zone addiction
of the now said 'stop' and the fields
once green grew overgrown.

The self remaindered itself,
met its image in a cul-de-sac
of confession and retreated
to a place without adjectives.

Not that it started you praying,
but it did make you a little blind.
Your handwriting grew large enough
to make out but not understand.

Now you make love to any man
with an echo of the 'only you'.
You forget their names as quickly
as the light goes out

and walk alone by the canal
to where you once lived.
That's what happens.
A life of wrong turns and detours

takes you away from where
you thought you were going.
Blame chance if you like.
Blame youth or the midday sun.

Blame Tantalus and the golden dog.
Whatever. The main thing is to remember
what you once had and pine,
go on, keep crying,

now you're the girl at the circus,
the one without her candy-floss.
Your grey eyes returned me
to where I am. Still bitter,

still mad, but not so dangerous to know,
no? The images you sell, if only
you worshipped them, bang on the doors
of your dreams. There's one

of a violin, or a man playing a violin,
two birds rest on his lap, the music
takes him above the city,
and away from the names

you once gave to their love.

Somewhere there's a river

what am I to do with this …
the impossibility of spring

what am I …
the cherry blossoms

fall and
                              fly
across the ground

they come towards me like
something from the past

all that longing
long forgot

I thought the muse
had left me

what is it you want from me anyway

my silence

but not before you seduced the moon
that night by the river
because somewhere
there is a river

and what of the cake
what are we like
some kind of Hansel and Gretel

not children
but be-forested and
hand in hand

we knew where we were going

we knew

nothing

what is it you want from me anyway

look somewhere there is a river

listen to the swans on its surface

they glide towards your hands

what is it you want from me

nothing

what is I want

everything

well then should we not have gone to the river
where the swans were waiting

where we fed them cake

I can't find anything

I should be beyond all of this

but no

it takes me
away
from where I should be

somewhere there's a river
meet me there

what can you remember of the night
do we forget
is it easier to forget

it's darkening
dark now

and the photographs
are they gone

what evidence do we need
to forgo the desire

somewhere there's a river
even the swans

if I close my eyes

what I remember is
your voice in the darkness
its gentle strangeness
to me
its tender appeal

what I remember is
meet me by the river

are you letting me go
have you let me go then

if I close my eyes

will the formality of the night be all
will ...

what I remember is your voice

If I ...

here the cherry blossoms
are falling like rain
like snow

like every drop of desire

they don't stop falling
they fall
and fall

bury me

in your hands
if I ...

cherry blossoms

and somewhere there's a river

and snow
your voice in the darkness

your hands
your
and
swans

swans
touch me too

Bull's tongue slumgullion

I.

bull's tongue slumgullion
gull fly onion bullion
slum tongue yum sum
tongue salad hum ya
curd roe red ho
strip tease please no
taxi man say so
no no knife life
tid bit what bit in it
bread ha well fed grave
stones grey stones no
bones burn tones
pig ears who hears
fear tears comrade dog
stop barking comrade
dog stop barking
harking and parking
your tongue's bull
slumgullion hungry
pumpkin drum coming
candle spigots
soviet spiddles
has dog comrade gone
doc what
sick you when when
slumgullion gulley cat
beggar beggar bye bye
what human nests
walk through

who who achoo
why what tank you
gesundheit it's my kite
slumgullion fly night
farewell out of sight
out of sight in mind
what mind my mind
mind gullion birch tree
tree climb
heim climb weh tune
home now hymn song
say so where to
here so
because

II.

and then I dreamt
no it was a nightmare
my fingers came unstuck
I gathered their bloody stumps
and announced the emergency to my wife
who shrugged
and continued to cut the wig
on our daughter's head
you are the only one
I know who will
have something to say
about these matters
write to me

Morning Song

decide one way or the other
        it's difficult you suppose

light hurts the eyes
        that have not slept

but stay in darkness
        and please no more sack cloth

the church is on its knees again
        no place for cupid

the only shrine is the one
        in my brother's room for Our Lady

images proliferate
        grow like mushrooms

the wax is heavy with pennies
        forget heaven

I'm talking about the poormouth
        who was your grandmother

and her dark faith
        the only music she heard

was the night drawing
        the curtain on itself

the doors are locked
       and morning is waiting

cupped in your hands
       like a blade of grass

your lips are blowing on to

only say the word

what we don't say to each other
                 is lost
                 somewhere
         in the soil
                 where tomorrow's   dog digs
         here's the bone
                 good boy
         juicy and bloody and fresh
everything said
         is screened
the words light up
                 when you walk through security
the way
         you walk
                 through
me
         and I become a host again
for all
         the rabbling   regret
of forgotten   gods

         above us   the sun
is
         ready
                         to
         fall
reach out
                 no
         your eyes   widen
at the possibility
                 of owning time again

but do you have the password

     it's like a sinking coin
         a promise
             laid   bare
     a memory
         dissolving
             in a glass of water

is your thirst slaked
     your philosophy true
     communicate
to me
     without words then
remake the sound
         with your eyes
         with your lips

                    remake me

Aubade

what love there is
is out of reach
sour rain and mint
leaves its history
in the air
but not for long
everything is disappearing
even the smell of you
marzipan desire sex
the distance between each word
wants nothing more
than its own
right to silence
I believe in
the folk-tale of pain
I believe
we will never
say these words
to one another again
salted lips
I'll have to relearn
an older language
don't bother thinking
of Carthage
Galway
how about Dublin
York Street
Number 9.3
sign here
general labourer
we will never say

these words again
tenements and memory
hiding in archives of rain
what apparitions
the moon dispels
are dream induced
and full of tears
we'll never talk
about the past
like we once did
the dry paper of our letters
is the kindle and lie
of early hearts
whatever the fortune tellers say
whatever your horoscope
predicts there'll be no record
save for the oblique
images of regret
and long-distance phone-calls
crows kept me company
on those dawn walks home
all time wants is a chance
to redeem itself
and pick the right colour
for its shroud
not a coloured coat
something white
and historical
children and intimates
are chasing the gods
we let go
eyes blur the words
meet me in the place
they have left

it's a gallery of flesh
a body without
the breath to say no

Love Poem

not eyes
don't start with the eyes
otherwise they will haunt you
besides you might say smoke
or water or winter
no eyes please

start with say her voice
or her name
or the way you met
and how everything changed from then on in

the gods gave way
and so on

another love poem
no
dahlia
a girl this time made sure of that
and some one else was watching
testing you I was she said

you failed
but won something

late nights
sex
free and fun filled
laughter-echoing sex

barefoot she came to the airport
sexy beast but tell her
when you cheat on her
she wants to know
and you do

no flower for that
no named flower
no name but the sigh of a disappointed traveller

this is where cupid comes asunder
fist in mouth arrow in foot
and all our wounds just deepened
love which once was scripted by your hand
is emailed now and dumped into the trash
deleted with no greek gods to conjure
no greek gods to conspire with
no classical allusions
no evocations or imaginings

Apollo can go and shite
and Mr. Graves keep bowing to the moon
love left you with regret

the shape of which might make an image

not floral
but empty open dark
and vegetative
with a hint of colour
from winter's end
bright then and expectant too
after all

Snow

Snow. All night. And
all day. Farms and in
the distance the sound
of an explosion to set
the avalanche off and
make it less a threat.

Morning's vast plain
cooling the face and
clearing the head.
The music from huts
rising like smoke.

Against the sky
clouds glide
like the silenced
desires of … snow.
On a branch a crow

calls out: what it says
is untranslatable.
Something to do with
the *sehnsucht* of a spring
day, something to do with love,

something to do with loss.

Nocturne

put your hand in this old hand
your lips to these drunken lips

wars are not your concern
fear not violence

I'll give you anything
let's drink

the sky opens for you
I can be your guide

take the darkness from me
you do

heal me
play the music you play

whisper to me again
of love

First Night

january is your month now
time of new beginnings
morning babe little flower

all day you gurgled
chirped and sang happiness
into our lives

as if we had not known
such a thing
as if we had been asleep

all our lives
as if
we had been but waiting

for this and how
you broke winter's yawn
with a yawlp

and gave a hundred names
to the shiver in the air
and the colours in the sky

as if
everything was done and undone
this very morning this very day

sung to and raised up
before so quickly the night arrived
and the hospital doors

closed to me
and so I thought
of how your heart-beat

slowed
before you were born
how frightened I was

before you were delivered
tugged-tired from your mother
how in counterpoint

my heart hurried
through the long-lived day
through the night

your first night
as I drove across the city
exiled from your swaddling

the steering-wheel brittle crumbling
and disappearing in my hands
commuted as I was

in some magical way
through the carnival
the medieval menagerie

to our first home
hungry thirsty elated and exhausted
where no one waited

cheered or cried
where the radio bleated
and the cats purred

where the newspapers grew stale
beneath my eyes
which fell closed

into sleep
o precious but wanton sleep
where I dreamt too of the image

of your new being
to where my heart began to sing
and to remake itself again anew

In the Spring of My Forty-first Year

I was never young or always was —
and was forever on my way

to becoming someone
whom I could sit or be silent with

running through Marlay Park
or up into Glencullen

with the rain on my face
my heart thirsting for nothing

no clock to keep time
no finish line either

the ease of distance in my legs
the breath bringing me

to who I am
away from the country

across time
to where we are

and back again to rough terrain
where I am no one nowhere

a figure in the evening
passing

my footfall ringing silently
through Pearse's Park

or Pine Forest or farther still
wordless and weightless

moving like the sun-scattered light
at once and irrevocably

towards you

NOTES

Many of the phrases in the title poem 'Gunpowder Valentine' are taken from Adi Roche's book *Chernobyl Heart* (New Island Books, 2006).

'Jesus as a young Hungarian deaf woman circa. 1940' is made up of words and phrases from *Deaf People in Hitler's Europe*, edited by Donna F. Ryan and John S. Schuchman (Gallaudet University Press, 2009). Part Three: The Jewish Deaf Experience, Deaf Survivors' Testimony: An Edited Transcript of *Klara Erdosi: Camp Experiences, Including Ravensbrück.*

In 'Gauguin on Three Rock', I have one eye on his painting 'Viriginity'.

Lightning Source UK Ltd.
Milton Keynes UK
UKHW020631150621
385545UK00012B/774